My Life's Story

by

Rev. Bud Robinson

First Fruits Press
Wilmore, Kentucky
2015

My Life's Story by Bud Robinson

Published by First Fruits Press, © 2015
Previously published by the Pentecostal Publishing Company, ©1906

ISBN: 9781621711988 (print), 9781621711971 (digital)

Digital version at
http://place.asburyseminary.edu/firstfruitsheritagematerial/95/

Robinson, Bud, 1860-1942.
    My life's story / by Bud Robinson.
    Third edition.
    217 pages : portrait; 21 cm.
    Wilmore, KY : First Fruits Press, ©2015.
    Reprint. Previously published: Kansas City, MO : Nazarene
    Publishing House, ©1928.
    ISBN: 9781621711988 (pbk.)
    1. Robinson, Bud, 1860-1942. 2. Church of the Nazarene –
    Clergy – Biography. 3. Clergy – United States – Biography. I.
    Title.
    BX8699.N38 2015   289.9

Cover design by Amelia Hegle

First Fruits Press
The Academic Open Press of Asbury Theological Seminary
204 N. Lexington Ave., Wilmore, KY 40390
859-858-2236
first.fruits@asburyseminary.edu
asbury.to/firstfruits

In Perfect Love:
Bird. Robinson.

MY LIFE'S STORY

BY

BUD ROBINSON

THIRD EDITION

NAZARENE PUBLISHING HOUSE
2923 Troost Ave., Kansas City, Mo.

1

My Life's Story

CHAPTER I

I was born in the mountains of Tennessee, in White County, on the 27th day of January, 1860, in an old log cabin with a dirt floor, a clapboard roof over our heads and a mud chimney about half way to the roof. We were in the very lowest depths of poverty. There was but one bedstead in the house, and it was not quartered oak, for the oak was not quartered. A little fork was put into the ground and one end of a pole into the fork and the other into the side of the house, and the bed was built on that scaffold. Our table was made the same way, of little oak boards.

There was not a window in the house, just one door, hung on the old wooden hinges and fastened with a latch which was opened by a string. No doubt the reader has heard of the latchstring hanging on the outside. The reading public ought to pay us something for that, as I think that must have started at our house. There was not a whole piece of furniture in the building. My mother cooked in the stewpot and baked in the old oven with a long-handled skillet. We generally ate out of tin pans, bucket lids, and with our fingers out of the skillet. That was not the worst part of it, for often we did not have enough to eat.

I have had people say, "Brother Bud, if you had just one bed, where did you all sleep? Were there many of you?"

I tell them, "No, there were not a great many, only mother and father and thirteen of us children."

People say, "Well, how in the world did you sleep?" When I was a boy we said we slept with our eyes shut. But people want to know how fifteen persons could sleep on one bed. Well, if you have never thrown a quilt on the floor and put boys on it and made them fit together like a package of teaspoons, you will never know how many you can put on one quilt. Many a night I have gone to bed hungry and my companion was the watchdog. I don't know which would growl the loudest—the dog or my stomach. The only trouble that I found sleeping with a dog was that you couldn't make him straighten out. He was the crookedest thing you ever saw when he lay down, unless it was the fellow he runs with.

In my childhood days, within five miles of our old cabin there were ten big distilleries. My father made apple brandy and sold it for fifty cents a gallon. He made whiskey and sold it for twenty-five cents a gallon, but it would make men just as drunk at that price as if they were paying a bootlegger ten dollars for it. The price of liquor doesn't seem to get the devil out of it, for men would swear just as loud when drunk on cheap whiskey as when they paid a big price for it; starve their wives and children and treat them just as bad. When a man tells you that he regrets that we are not back in the days of cheap whiskey, you might tell him that every day he stays away from the insane asylum he is going to be away from home, for I was brought up on cheap whiskey.

In those days everybody became drunk when a young couple were married or someone died. In the winter time they had whiskey to warm them up so they could roll logs. In the summer time they had whiskey to cool them off, so they could cut wheat. When people were sick they gave them whiskey to make them well. When they were well, they gave them whiskey to keep them from getting sick. So the reader will see at a glance that we used it for all purposes.

In those days, my father ran what was commonly called a grocery, which was nothing more nor less than a country saloon. They were generally located in an old log house at the fork of the road. Here our neighbors would meet and would often get up a shooting match, bring their old rifles and shoot for whiskey until they would all get drunk and then the fighting would begin. I have known them to make a big ring about ten feet across, pull off their shirts and tie their galluses around their waists, and sometimes fight for an hour, and beat each other until they were bloody. I have seen my dear old father come home with his head beaten up and his face bloody, and swear so bitterly at my mother that I would stand and tremble, while the little children would hide.

I have heard people say that they didn't believe in a devil. I know there is one because he lived at our house. If there is such a thing as a hell on earth, it's the home of a poor drunkard, for he is without God and generally without money, without clothing and almost without food. I have known men unable to buy clothing for their families and the necessities of life, but I have never known a drunkard but what could get liquor and tobacco. They are the twin evils. We now have thousands of boys in our penitentiaries and schools of correction. The devil, liquor and tobacco have put every one of them there.

I have often thought of the little boy who was walking down the street and saw a drunken man lying at the door of the saloon. The little fellow walked to the door of the saloon, hailed the saloonkeeper and said, "Mister, your billboard fell down and I came to tell you in order that you could stand it up again." But that is only one case among hundreds and thousands that our nation has produced.

I want to stop right here long enough to say that every bootlegger in the United States ought to be captured and if he is a foreigner, he ought to be sent back to his native land, with the understanding that he could never enter America again; and if he is American born, he should be sentenced to the state penitentiary for ten years. During that time he ought to be made to build public roads for the sober people to drive over. I think bootleggers have forfeited their rights to freedom and liberty in this great country of ours.

Well, after making this little detour, we are back at the little log cabin on the mountain side. Before the death of my father, my older brothers were getting drunk every week, lying in the yard so drunk they couldn't walk and my oldest sisters were old enough to receive company. Now the next question was, what kind of company would they keep? Well, as the reader knows, it is customary for the boys and girls as a rule, to marry the boys and girls they run with. But the young men that came to our house were so drunk they couldn't get off their ponies. We would help them down and bring them in, but they would be so drunk that they could not introduce a courtship. We would then throw down an old quilt and they would lie down and sleep off the drunk, wake up, go out by the old spring, wash their faces, wipe them off on a gunny sack, and if they combed their hair (I have seen them straighten it out with a mule currycomb) come in and start their courtship.

I have had people say, "Brother Bud, you people must have been mighty low down." Well, the reader can see at a glance that we needed God and somebody to help us. Many people who made fun of my grammar never gave a nickel during their lives to help educate me. While we were low down, I judge we were just about on a par with the rest of our neighbors. The reader must remember that the great Cumberland mountain range of Tennessee sixty years ago, where they were without churches and without schools but with plenty of stillhouses, was by no means a paradise. I have been in the homes of some of our mountain people where the mother of the house would have six or eight children, the oldest daughter would have two or three, the next oldest from one to two, and then the younger girls were already wrecked. But nobody seemed to care.

The last time I was through those mountains, I stood on the spots where the old stillhouses used to be and could locate a half dozen places where men had been killed. The last time I preached in those mountains (just a few years ago), two young men fought in the door of the church and they were so badly cut up with their knives that one of them was carried off on a stretcher. One of the young men that started the fuss at that time had a brother in the penitentiary in Nashville, Tennessee, for murder. So the reader can see that even down to the present there is a great need of revival of old-fashioned, heart-felt, Holy Ghost religion in that mountain range.

Before the death of my father I was old enough to go to mill as we called it. The corn was shelled and put in a sack which was placed on the pony. I was then placed on the sack of corn and sent a number of miles to the old water mill, where the corn was ground into meal. It was necessary for each one to await his turn and while our corn was grinding, we boys would play marbles, play in the little creek, place the little fish in the pens built of rocks and have lots of fun.

It was at the old mill that I met another little boy who seemed to love me, and often would ask me to come to his home and stay all night. Finally my mother gave her consent. I walked about twelve miles through the mountains following the pig trails. I was dirty, ragged and barefooted. As the ground was very cold, it was a harder trip than going to New York from Los Angeles, California, by rail. I reached their home about sundown. It was a very large hewn-log house with a puncheon floor, a big rock chimney, a broad stone hearth and a big fireplace. They had on the big backlog, the forestick and the middle wood. There was a row of big, fat feather beds around the walls. Their big, hewn-log kitchen, with a puncheon floor and a big rock chimney, contained a long table with a beautiful, white tablecloth on it together with plates, cups and saucers, knives and forks, and, best of all, there was plenty to eat. When we sat down to eat everything was so nice and quiet. The old father turned his face toward heaven and offered thanks. I had never heard that before, therefore did not know what he was doing. I thought he was talking to somebody in the room. I tried to locate the person he was talking to. It was the most beautiful thing I had ever heard. When the blessing was asked he began to fill the plates. He piled good things on them until they were full and then passed them around to the family. When he came to my plate he piled good things on it until it could hold no more. It looked and smelled so good that I did not want to eat it. I wanted to smell of it, taste of it, and then put it away for a keepsake. I was afraid that I would never get anything else like it again. But I watched the boys wade into their supper and the next thing I had my supper wading into me. I ate up what was on my plate and the old man put on another spoonful and then he piled on some more and finally I came to the end, but he piled on another spoonful and said, "My little man, would you eat a little more?" All that I could do was to look up with a grin and say, "Well, I might chaw a little more but I can't swallow any more."

After the good supper was finished, the family moved into the big parlor. Of course it was not like the parlor of the homes in our days but after traveling for a million miles, I have not seen a greater parlor than that one. It is true that all the beds were in one room, but the reader must remember that was customary in the mountains in those days. The mother and father sat down and entered into a conversation as though they loved each other, while the children entertained the little, dirty saloonkeeper's boy. First, we had a great rousing game of blindfold. My, my, but that was exciting! When that was over, we roasted potatoes and played a game called "Clubfist." You never saw the like of the fun we had that night! When that was over we played a game called "Chick-a-ma-cranie-crow." That was the most exciting game I had ever seen or heard of. My, we mighty near moved the house! But after that was over the old father told the boys to go into the cellar and bring up a big bucket of apples. They were the old "Mountain Reds," commonly called "Limber Twigs." They were a great apple and smelled so good that one of them almost perfumed the settlement. I think I ate apples until I could reach them with my finger. I am sure they came up above Adam's apple.

After eating apples, the old father said, "Children, it is bedtime," and every child quit playing and sat down on the floor and turned his feet toward the big fireplace. The old father sat over by a little table with a little tallow candle in the candlestick. Even now I can see the glimmering light of the little tallow candle as the old father pulled a big book over on his lap. I had no idea that they were going to have family worship. As I couldn't read, I have no idea what the old man read.

Just for a moment I will skip over and tell you that many years later I was converted on the frontiers of Texas. Three months after my conversion I attended my first Sunday school, where a young lady gave me a nickel Testament which I learned to read. A year later I bought a Bible and in reading it through, came to that beautiful thirty-fifth chapter of Isaiah's prophecy. Of course, I don't know whether that is the chapter the old man read or not, but it sounded very much like it, and even if it was not the one he read, it was my experience. Out there on the great plains of Texas, forty-seven years ago, as I was reading my Bible by the sunshine by day and by moonshine at night, with my boyish heart overflowing with love for God and everybody on earth, I could look beyond the great plains of Texas, across Arkansas and western Tennessee, and see the big hewn-log house on the top of the Cumberland mountains. I could see that rugged old mountaineer with his shaggy beard, his long brown hair combed back on his shoulders. I could see his wife sitting by him and the seven or eight children sitting on the puncheon floor, with their bare feet turned toward the big fire. I could hear him reading:

"The wilderness and the solitary place shall

be glad for them; and the desert shall rejoice, and blossom as the rose.

"It shall blossom abundantly, and rejoice even with joy and singing: the glory of Lebanon shall be given unto it, the excellency of Carmel and Sharon, they shall see the glory of the Lord, and the excellency of our God.

"Strengthen ye the weak hands, and confirm the feeble knees.

"Say to them that are of a fearful heart, Be strong, fear not: behold, your God will come with vengeance, even God with a recompence; he will come and save you.

"Then the eyes of the blind shall be opened, and the ears of the deaf shall be unstopped.

"Then shall the lame man leap as an hart, and the tongue of the dumb sing: for in the wilderness shall waters break out, and streams in the desert.

"And the parched ground shall become a pool, and the thirsty land springs of water: in the habitation of dragons, where each lay, shall be grass with reeds and rushes.

"And an highway shall be there, and a way, and it shall be called The way of holiness; the unclean shall not pass over it; but it shall be for those: the wayfaring men, though fools, shall not err therein.

"No lion shall be there, nor any ravenous beast shall go up thereon, it shall not be found there; but the redeemed shall walk there:

"And the ransomed of the Lord shall return, and come to Zion with songs and everlasting joy upon their heads: they shall obtain joy and gladness, and sorrow and sighing shall flee away."

When he had finished reading this beautiful chapter, he laid the Bible on the table and they all knelt in prayer. I had no idea what they were doing, but I knelt with them. He prayed for his wife as though he loved her and called her by name and seemed to hold her right up to the throne of grace. Then one by one he prayed for every child he had, calling them by name, asking God for His love and mercy to be thrown around his family, pleading with God to protect them from evil, harm and danger. He did not forget the little, dirty, ragged saloonkeeper's boy. He began to pray for me and asked God to take that little boy and save him from sin and fill him with the Holy Spirit and make him a blessing to his family. Then he asked God to take that boy and make him a blessing to the world. My little heart was breaking as I broke down and began to weep.

Although I was a little, dirty, ragged boy of twelve years, I began to make some good resolutions. I said, "Some day I am going to be as big as this man, and I am going to have a home, a wife and children. I am also going to have a big, long table with a white tablecloth on it, with plenty of good things to eat. When we sit down to eat, I am going to look up and talk to somebody and when supper is over I am going to play blindfold with my children. Well, beloved, I lived to see all those desires fulfilled. After I was married and

God had given me two beautiful babies, I would go out and evangelize, come home and there find the long table with its white tablecloth and plenty to eat. We could look up and thank the heavenly Father for the good things of life. Then when supper was over, I would pull off my coat and tie an old towel over our eyes. My tots and I would have a great game of blindfold. The reader can see that a little boy may plan to do something good and live to see it fulfilled.

That night in the old mountain home, after the old father had said Amen, he led me back to a big fat feather bed, took off some of my dirty clothes and rolled me into a bed that seemed to be knee-deep in goose feathers. It just seemed to me that I was wallowing in goose feathers and could almost hear the geese saying that they had had their feathers pulled off in order to make me a bed. Then he pulled a big woolen blanket up around my neck (one of those old homespun blankets). My, my, how warm it was! The wool was so long that it tickled my neck. I have often thought I could hear the lamb bleat, "My wool has been sheared to make the blanket with which you are covered." Of course I had heard about the goodness and the love of God. That night I thought I was in God's house. Dear reader, I don't think I was very much amiss for I verily believe that God dwelt in the home of that old mountaineer.

I am sure that I enjoyed a good night's sleep, for the first thing I knew, he was calling us to breakfast. We boys were soon up, our faces washed, and served with a good breakfast, after which the old mountaineer called his family around the family altar and had morning worship and prayers. He took a big old grubbing-hoe and swung his chopping axe over his shoulder, striding across his farm to the back side where he was clearing land. I can hear him as he went across the farm singing, "Jesus, Lover of my soul, let me to thy bosom fly." I thought it was the most beautiful song I had ever heard.

I was soon wending my way across the mountains to my old home, but not for a minute was I satisfied. I had experienced something better and had seen something better. I am sure of one thing and that is: there is not a happy backslider in the world, for no one that has enjoyed something better than he now has can ever be happy. Therefore, after I had spent one night in a Christian home where they had plenty to eat, good beds to sleep on and family prayers, I could not go back to the shack of a moonshiner and be happy again.

A great while after that my father was on his death bed. He was then sixty years of age and his life had not been what it ought to have been. When he came to die he said, "I can't die. Out there is the blackest world that a man has ever seen. I can't go out into the darkness. It is blacker than Egypt. Go and find someone to pray for me." A man was found who came and prayed for my dying father. He thought before he died that the light of heaven had come into his heart and the burden was gone. Beloved, I do hope and trust that my poor father was saved during his last hours, but sometimes I feel sad when I think of it, because the Bible tells us to try every spirit and see whether it be of God. The Book says the devil can transform himself into an angel of light. I have feared sometimes that my poor father was unsaved, he could not try the spirit to see whether it was of God and the devil might have come in his dying moment as an angel of light and deceived him. But oh, beloved, I do hope and trust that he is saved.

And now, dear reader, let me plead with you, if you are unsaved, for the sake of your precious, immortal soul, do not put off the salvation of your soul until you come to your death bed, for Jesus Christ said, "What shall it profit a man if he shall gain the whole world if he loses his own soul?" Let the reader remember that when Jesus spoke about our soul he put the world in the balance and said our soul outweighed the world. Then, beloved reader, isn't it strange that a man would sell his soul for naught? But whether ready or not, he passed out.

CHAPTER II

My mother was restless in those mountains, a hundred miles from a railroad, fifteen miles from a post-office, many miles to the old water mill, without churches and schools. The three older children left home, left mother and ten fatherless, poverty-stricken children. My father died in 1872, but in 1876 my mother decided to leave the mountains of Tennessee and migrate to Texas where her children would have a better opportunity. She sold out what little she was possessed of, a few ponies, cows, a flock of sheep, a few shotes, household utensils, and a field of corn. She went ten miles to get a man to bring his wagon and mules to haul her and her ten children to Nashville. We were three days and nights making the trip of one hundred miles.

We left the mountains on Tuesday morning, September 12, 1876; six days later we landed in the city of Dallas, Texas. We were three days on the road, coming to Nashville and three days going from Nashville to Dallas.

Fifty-two years ago Dallas was only a straggling village on the banks of the Trinity river. I think there were more saloons and gambling places in Dallas than any other kind of business houses, for Dallas was the headquarters (in those days) for most of the people that came west. The reader knows that Dallas has

17

now become a great city. Most of the traveling fifty years ago was by mule or ox wagons.

A large number of people coming to Texas were mere squatters who would pick up a homestead consisting of 160 acres of land, stay on it a short time and then pull up and return to Arkansas, Louisiana or Tennessee, and within a year or two would come back. I have known people to make eight and ten trips between Texas and Arkansas. They used to come from Arkansas in their old ox wagons, called prairie schooners, on one side of which was written, "I am a rackin' from Rackensack, going to Texas or bust." The next year they would come back and written on the other side of the sheet was "I am a rackin' back to Rackensack—busted." I have seen eight and ten wagons in one company. They would strike camp, sit around the campfire at night, smoke their old cob pipe and some would cuss Texas and brag on Arkansas, while others would cuss Arkansas and brag on Louisiana. Then others would cuss Louisiana and brag on Oklahoma, but finally some old fellow would light his old cob pipe, rear back on his old rawhide bottom chair, let out a mouth full of smoke, and say, "Now boys, hear me. You will never be able to get all the coons up one tree." He was the philosopher of the crowd. He meant by not getting all the coons up one tree, they would not get them all to agree on one state.

But those were wonderful days in the settling of the great plains of Texas. When in 1876 we landed in that part of the country, there were very few engaged in farming. It was a great stock country. You could ride for a hundred miles and scarcely see a house, nothing but horses and cattle as far as you could see. The men wore leather breeches, a big linsey shirt and broad-brimmed white hats with leather bands around them. They wore high-heeled boots, big pairs of spurs, and most of them had a six shooter buckled on them.

We were not out there long before mother put me to work on a little farm or stock ranch. The man and his wife were Universalists and preached universal doctrines. According to their theology, God brought them into the world without their consent and He would take them out without their permission, therefore if He was a merciful God, as He claimed to be, He would be in duty bound to take them to heaven. During the first week I was in their home, they taught me to play cards. A few nights later they had a big country dance. The man's wife took me by the hand and led me out on the floor, taking me through my first eight-handed country dance.

It wasn't long before the man and his brothers ran a horse race as they owned a race mare. They took me to the race, which in the early days of Texas was very exciting for a young man. Hundreds of men with six shooters buckled on their belts which were full of gold, would pile up a great number of twenty dollar gold pieces and would tell the rider if he didn't ride the horse for all that was in him, he would get a bullet right through his head. Dear reader, just imagine one of the riders, who was nothing more than a half grown boy, racing his mount with the understanding that if he didn't ride the horse for everything that he could get out of him, there would be a bullet put through his head. While it was gambling under the direct control and operation of the devil, yet in one sense it was honest gambling. That is, the horse that could outrun the other would win the gold. You can picture a poor boy like myself at a country dance, playing cards, or attending a horse race. It would not be long until he would be going the downward grade.

For four years we lived that kind of a life until we became as wild as antelopes. But my old mother had been saved in the meantime and she was praying for her boy. Late one afternoon we heard somebody singing and upon looking up saw a man riding a gray pony. He came up and said that he was a Methodist circuit rider, and had come to stay all night. When I came close to him, my heart had all kinds of spells. Sometimes it would run so fast that it would flutter and then it would stand still and wouldn't go at all. When he told me to put up his horse, water and feed him, I trembled from head to foot. I was afraid to ride the horse to water, for fear he would fall down and kill me and then I knew the devil would get me. Finally the horse was watered and fed. The boys had planned a game of seven-up for that night, but we haven't played that game as yet and I am of the opinion that the game will never be played.

We went out to supper, sat down and commenced eating but he said, "Hold on there, young men, we are going to ask a blessing at this table." Everything was as still as death and the eyes of the old Universalist fairly bulged out as the old man turned his face toward heaven and returned thanks. In a moment of time my mind went back to the old hewn-log house in the mountains, where the rugged, old mountaineer had said grace at his table when I was a little boy. After the preacher said grace, all the boys went to eating as if in a hurry. He seemed to understand and he said, "Young men, don't leave when supper is over until we have family prayers." My, my! Think of having family prayers in one of those ranch cabins where the branding iron and lariat were lying near the door, six shooters hanging around the wall and the Winchester rifles stacked in the corner. But nevertheless, when the old preacher gave orders, we obeyed.

Supper being ended, he opened up his saddle-bags, brought out his Bible and read a long chapter about heaven. When he called us to prayer, every one of us went down on our knees. The reader can see the difference between playing seven-up and two-down. That's the reason we never played the game, as seven-up is played with a deck of cards and two-down is played on the knees. The old preacher didn't ask us how long he would be permitted to pray, nor how loud, nor what he was to tell the Lord. No, beloved, he did not consult us, but when he began to pray you could hear him for a quarter of a mile. He prayed as loud as he could whoop. It seemed to me he knew everything we had done for four years, and told the Lord about it. He told Him we were out there drinking, gambling, lying and stealing and that there was just one breath between us and the hot doors of damnation. It was so awful that I would get so cold that my teeth would chatter; then I would get so hot that the perspiration would break out all over me. As the old man continued in prayer he would shout at the top of his voice: "Great God, keep these men out of hell tonight."

Beloved, that was one long night. At about the break of day, the old preacher awoke, rolled out of his bunk, went down on his knees and prayed. After dressing he went out about the barn to have his morning worship and secret prayer. While he was supposed to have been praying in secret, you could hear him all over the place. Breakfast was soon ready and he offered thanks again, read another chapter and had prayer with us. After saddling his horse, he brought his saddlebags and his Bible and mounted the gray pony. We could hear him as he went across the plains, singing in a loud, clear voice, "Amazing grace, how sweet the sound, that saved a wretch like me. I once was lost, but now I am found, was blind but now I see." The one thing I never shall forget was that when he was getting ready to mount the pony, he shook hands with us and held onto our hands until they ached and said so kindly, "My friends, I can't get back to see you for a month." No one had asked him to return but nevertheless we stood and watched as he rode away and heard the last words of that beautiful old hymn float across the prairie. Just as the sun was rolling up from behind the eastern hills, while he was singing the last verse of "Amazing Grace, How Sweet the Sound," over in a ravine located about a half mile from the ranch, a great pack of wolves set up a howl until it seemed like they would wake up the dead. What a strange feeling came over us. God's messenger singing a beautiful old hymn while the wolves were howling until the ground fairly shook. Though I was not saved, and did not know God, it seemed to me that Jesus Christ had come to the frontier of Texas, in the life of this preacher, and that the devil was in a pack of wolves, and the devil was fleeing before Christ. I suppose that in all uncivilized and unsettled countries the wolves howl by day and by night. Beloved reader, no country is civilized or settled until the preacher of the gospel appears on the scene. Whether you agree with me or not, a country has progressed a long way toward civilization when the preacher of the gospel arrives on the scene.

Sure enough, one afternoon about a month later, we heard a song and saw the old gray pony coming back to the stock ranch. The man of God had made his circuit. But oh, beloved, how different from the first time he came. When he arrived the second time, the whole crowd was down at the gate to shake hands and give him a hearty welcome. It felt as though God had come to the frontier. After shaking hands he gave us some bad news. Well, some of you may say, "What was the bad news? Had any of his loved ones died? Had some misfortune befallen him?" Oh, no, beloved, it was worse than that. He said, "I am going to stay with you two or three days on this trip." My, my, my, my heart sank within me as I said to myself, "If this preacher stays here three days, I will be a dead man, for no man can stand his praying for three days." Sure enough, for the next two or three days he prayed in the house, in the barn, behind the haystack and out in the ravine. Any time of the day or night you could hear the man in prayer. All the praying he did at the house was called family prayers, but when he was praying behind the haystack so you could hear him for a half mile, he called it secret prayer. The reader will agree with me that nowadays we need someone to have secret prayer and pray so loud that it will alarm the settlement. That man will never know how much good he accomplished on that trip. For it was his praying in secret, as he called it, that stirred every fiber of my being, until my very soul was alarmed over my condition.

Before he left, he told us he was going to hold a campmeeting about eighteen or twenty miles below where we lived. It was to be held during the month of August in the year 1880. My mother planned to go to that campmeeting with one of our neighbors in his mule wagon. Mother told me she was going to take me with her. When the time came to go to meeting I climbed down from a Texas saddle, threw down a lariat and a branding iron and pulled off my spurs. I did not change my clothes for if I had, I would have gone without any. I had on every rag of clothing that I possessed, consisting of an old pair of gray overalls with the knees out, an old, dirty, blue hickory shirt with the elbows out, and an old pair of run-down boots with the toes out. I had neither socks nor coat to put on. I wore an old, dirty, white hat with a leather band on it. It was so greasy it would have made soap. That was my Sunday suit and my everyday clothes.

My old preacher friend was instrumental in getting a rich old ranchman converted who told the preacher that if he would arrange for an old Methodist camp-meeting like they used to have in the North when he was a boy, they could kill as many of his fat cattle as were needed to make beef. He had them scattered over the plains for hundreds of miles. People living at a distance of 250 miles came to the meeting in their ox wagons. In those days the wagons were covered with old-fashioned sheets and bows which made a roof over their heads.

The men dug a big trench and put on a big wash-kettle for stewing beef. They would then go out and kill a big fat calf and put it in the kettle and stew it while the women baked big old brown-back biscuits in the skillets over the chunk fires. The biscuits had brown backs and white hearts and were so good that if a fellow should eat one he would never forget it. They made coffee in the tea-kettles. They would put big pans of biscuits on the tables which were a hundred feet long and about three feet wide, together with big bowls of stewed beef and pour the black coffee into pint cups. The people would line up on both sides of the table, sing a song and say grace. I have seen the old mothers shout until they would shake their bonnets off and the tucking combs from their hair. No charge was made for the meals. They were free to everyone.

Deep conviction had settled down on me the second day. I felt that I was lost. One day the preachers asked the workers to go down into the crowd and find a sinner and pray for him wherever they found him. A beautiful old mother with beautiful white hair and the finest face I ever saw came through the crowd. She looked like you could take a rag and wipe heaven off her face. She found me sitting on the back bench. There was no need of her saying, "Young man, are you a sinner?" She looked at me and knew no Christian ever looked like I did. She went down before me on her knees and put her hands upon my bare knees where they were sticking through my dirty overalls and prayed for me as loud as she could. The devil got up and said, "If you don't give her a cussing she never will quit." But it seemed the Lord said, "Don't you cuss this woman, she is praying for your lost soul." Then it seemed to me that the devil said, "If you don't get up and run they are going to get you." But beloved, God had come on the scene. I tried to get up but could not get off the bench. It seemed as though I was glued to it while the devil fairly hissed in my face. That beautiful mother prayed louder and louder and finally began to shout and rising on her knees began to beat me on the head until I thought I was going to sink through the ground into the pit. The old mother shouted as long as she wanted to and when she finally arose, looked like she was half glorified. She went back toward the platform and mourner's bench but she did not say when she left, "Young man, come to the altar tonight." No, beloved, she did not ask me to come to the altar. That woman was acquainted with God and knew I was coming to the mourner's bench provided I ever was able. That was the only thing to be considered.

When the service was over, I finally pulled loose from that bench and arose but the arrow of conviction had gone through my poor heart until I couldn't pull it out. In my agony I walked the grounds that afternoon, too sick to eat my dinner. I wished for the sun to go down. I thought if the sun would go down that it would get dark and no one could see how mean I was. When the sun went down my awful heart was not only dark on the outside but it was black on the inside. Then I felt that I would be a dead man before daylight. But, praise the Lord, they lit up the old torch-lights on the ground and the congregation began to sing, "Oh, who will come and go with me, I'm bound for the promised land." I marched up to the camp ground and had taken a back seat when I noticed a little red-headed girl that I had met somewhere on the dance floor. The devil always goes to meeting. He came to me and said, "If you can get up a courtship with that little girl on the back bench you will get easy." But beloved, a courtship never eases a guilty conscience and a lost soul. While I tried to talk to her, I felt like a lost man.

The preacher who had preached up to that night was a tall man with a long beard and hair a little inclined to baldness and wore a long coat. The man who preached that night did not fill the bill as far as I was concerned. He wore a very short coat. His beard was short and his hair stood straight up on his head. He looked dangerous. I thought he couldn't preach a lick and would be a failure. I later learned that he was one of the greatest preachers west of the Mississippi river.

He preached of a lost world without a Savior, where the devil was boss and general manager, and where people were under the awful dominion of the devil. He pictured Christ laying aside His robes of royal splendor, putting on humanity, and being born in a manger; then he pictured Christ on the cross, because He loved a lost and dying world. He made the crucifixion of Christ so real that it seemed to me He had died a week ago somewhere in Texas.

When he made his altar call, the response was so general that to all appearance the whole crowd would finally land at the altar. They went whooping, yelling, screaming and praying just as loud as they could. Two or three preachers were helping men to the altar. There were so many that they turned the benches around to make a great big pen. They actually filled it full. I stood back and wept. I wanted to go to the altar but as I knew nothing of church, preachers, meetings or salvation, I really did not know how to start or what to do.

Thank God, He will always help the boy that wants to do right. An old preacher with long white beard and beautiful white locks came down the aisle and said, "Is there a young man back here that wants to meet me in heaven?" If so, come and give me your hand and I will pray that God may save you." I stood and wept. One moment I said, "If Jesus loved me well enough to die for me, I will love Him well enough to fight for Him." While in the next breath, I said, "I will shoot the first man that talks about Jesus Christ." My gun, which was loaded, was in my pocket. As the old preacher pleaded I started, saying, "I can do that much, I can at least give him my hand." When I reached him I was crying as loud as I could. He grabbed at my hand, missed it, but took me by the arm. He gave it a shake and when he turned me loose, I started down the aisle toward the mourner's bench. I did not go very far until the devil stood before me and said, "If you go to the mourner's bench, the preacher will see your ragged old breeches and make fun of you." When he couldn't stop me with that, he said, "They'll see your old pistol and that will get you into trouble." But, thank God, he didn't stop me with that, but as I went down the aisle the old pistol felt as big as a mule; and the old deck of cards in my pocket was as big as a bale of cotton. When I would get on my right foot, I thought I was going right into the pit and I would stagger. Then when I would get on my left foot, that deck of cards weighed as much as a bale of cotton. I know today exactly what King David meant when he said, "They will reel to and fro, and will stagger like a drunken man and be at their wit's end."

When I reached the altar, somebody said, "Fix a seat for this young man. He is deeply struck." Thank God, that man was a philosopher. The only mistake he made, was that I was not able to sit in a rocking chair because my hide was so full of gospel bullets that I was just about all in. I fell over the mourner's bench and somebody got me by the heels and straightened me out. Right there I caught the devil in a lie. He told me when I started down the aisle that those people

would see my old ragged breeches and make fun of me.
To my glad surprise, every preacher knelt around me
as I prayed and screamed as loud as I could, for God
to have mercy on me and save my lost soul. My
shrieks and wails seemed to touch the heart of every
preacher there as they knelt around me with their faces
turned toward heaven and their hands in the air. I had
never heard men pray like that before.

It was a life and a death struggle. A poor soul was
right on the borderland of death and destruction, but
God's mercy had reached my case. While we were
praying together the bottom dropped out of heaven and
my soul was flooded with light and joy until literal
waves of glory rolled up and down my soul. I don't
know how I got up, but bless God, I know I got up
because I am up now. When I did get on my feet, the
people looked like angels. They appeared to be robed
in white. It was as light as if it had been at the noon
hour of the day but behold it was about eleven o'clock
at night. This was on Wednesday, August 11, 1880.
How well I recall that night. It will stay with me
forever. No doubt the reader has heard the little song,
"How well I remember in sorrow's dark night, when
the lamp of His word shed its beautiful light, more
grace He has given and the burden's removed, and over
and over His goodness I've proved. And shall I turn
back into the world? Oh, no, not I, not I."

I believe that getting religion is the finest thing in
the known world. After I hopped, skipped, jumped
and shouted until midnight, I would jump the mourner's bench from one side to the other, all the time

telling the people that I had got religion. Well, thank the Lord, I got religion sure enough, and it seemed like religion had got me. After shouting until about midnight, I went down to the ravine and threw my revolver away. I kindled a little chunk fire and burnt my deck of cards. Then I crawled under an ox wagon, lay down on the bare ground, and placed my hat on a chunk for a pillow. I did not go to sleep, for sleep had left the country. I lay there and laughed like a boy at a circus. I was almost tickled to death—every burden gone, my guilt gone and all sorrow and sadness gone. I forgot that I lived in poverty. I thought that I was dressed like the angels. While my heart was turning somersaults, I was laughing like a boy at a circus. I was one boy that kept company with his religion the very first night that he got it. I felt that night as though I never would be sick, sad, lonesome, hungry or in trouble. It seemed to me that heaven was three feet away.

During the night Jesus came under the wagon and called me to preach. I could see His beautiful face with a crown of thorns on His brow. I could see the sweat and blood mingled on His face, and the old purple robe over His shoulders. He was so real to me. I can never forget my first meeting with Jesus. He told me that He wanted me to preach His gospel while I told Him that I would go. I had no idea, that night, what it meant to be a God-called preacher of the gospel, but after forty-seven years of preaching almost day and night, living a lonely life, sometimes spending only one week at home during a whole year, I have found that when God calls a man to preach, God really has something for him to do.

The night He called me to preach I saw no evening slippers, and no smoking gowns, no cigar cases, and no easy hammock, but I saw a world steeped in sin, sin-cursed, devil-ridden, hell-plodding and without hope. But thank God, His grace has never failed. I believe the Book, "My grace is sufficient for thee. Your strength is made perfect in weakness. I will uphold thee with the right hand of my righteousness. I will guide thee with mine eye." I believe the preacher that is led by the spirit of the Master, upheld by the right hand of His righteousness, and guided with His eye, will get to the right place every time, and also get there at the right time. Beloved, I believe that you ought to ask God to help us, as preachers of the gospel, to do the right thing at the right time and do the thing in the right way.

The next morning, as day was beginning to break, I crawled from under the ox wagon and went out on the camp ground. I watched the sun rise in all its grandeur and glory. The whole heavens were lighted up. I would look in one direction and it would appear to be like mountains of oranges; in another direction, like tons of strawberries and I'd look in another direction and it was like tons of ice cream. It seemed to me that the angels were having strawberries and ice cream for breakfast. I turned and looked at a great flock of clouds in another direction and it had the appearance of a great flock of sheep with their wool on fire. Just about that time heaven came down to the earth and I was so blest that soon I was leaping up and down, clapping my hands and praising God as loud as I could shout.

About that time a man came along and said, "Are you going up to the testimony meeting this morning?" I said, "Yes, sir, I am going up." I had never been in a testimony meeting. In fact I had never heard tell of one. As I walked up to the big arbor, I wondered what kind of meeting it would be. If it was as good as the one we had last night, it would surely be great. When we got up to the arbor the man took down a big ox horn and blew until it sounded like a bugle. They used the ox horn instead of a bell to call the people to the tabernacle. At the sound of that horn the people came from every direction. They came out of their wagons and tents until there were people all over the old camp shed. A man read a few verses of scripture; they sang and prayed, after which the meeting was open for testimonies. I wondered what in the world it was going to be like.

A man arose and began to praise God and testify to the saving grace of God. While he testified my heart was leaping for joy, but when he sat down, another man beat me up. A big tall man with black beard and long black hair with a big woolen shirt, overalls and high-heeled boots, stood in the presence of that crowd. His frame trembled as he said, "Oh, brethren, I have been on these prairies for twenty years as a ranchman and have committed all the sins known to a ranchman. When I heard of this meeting last night about dark it made me mad. I saddled my horse and rode in last

night. I came to whip every preacher on the grounds
and run everybody off. But when I arrived here last
night at a late hour, I beheld one of the strangest sights
of my life. There would be a crowd over on one side
singing, and a crowd on another side shouting. Their
hands were up; their hair was hanging down their
backs and their faces looked like angels. Over in another place would be a crowd down on their knees
praying. Somebody would then rise up and start
shouting. I said, 'Well, I won't whip anybody until
they quit and quiet down,' but instead of stopping,
they became worse. Finally (to see just what they
were doing), I made my way through the crowd to a
bench right in the middle of the arbor where I could
see everything that was going on. The great multitude
seemingly did not know I was there but while they
prayed, sang and shouted, my whole life stood before
me. I saw that I was a lost man. I knew that if I
should die I would go straight to hell. The burden
became so awful that I fell off the bench. I got down
between two benches where two or three men gathered
around me. They began to sing and pray with and for
me. This morning, just before day, God saved my
soul."

I could stand it no longer. I had to do something
or die or simply blow up. I jumped just as high as I
could; screamed as loud as I could and began to jump
up and down as fast as I could. It looked like I would
die with religious satisfaction. The Lord came to my
relief and showed me a big post under the old arbor. I
threw both arms around that post and started up just

like a gray squirrel. I climbed until my head got to the brush and I could go no farther. While I was sticking there on the side of the post, God poured out His Spirit on the people.

After forty-seven years of preaching on the greatest camp grounds of the nation, I have yet to witness another such scene as took place there on that morning. I believe that the Holy Spirit was poured out on that multitude of from 150 to 300 people and they were filled with the Holy Ghost just as they were on the day of Pentecost. There were hundreds of people leaping in the air clapping their hands, praising God at the top of their voice. Men ran into each other's arms and wrestled like athletes. The women literally danced and shouted until they looked like angels. Waves of glory swept over them until it looked like they were immersed in glory. Of course, I could not stay on the side of the post long and had to climb down. I got down on the bench and watched them.

After the glory had subsided, the preacher said they would open the doors of the church this morning. Then I wondered again what they were going to do. I could not see how they could open the doors of the church when there was no church in sight. They stood up and sang, "Amazing Grace, how sweet the sound," to the tune of the old southern melody. My! My! What music they made. While they sang the old hymn, a great multitude marched up and gave the preacher their hands, and I saw what it meant to open the doors of the church.

Being led of the Spirit, I marched up and gave the

preacher my hand. He took me by the hand and with such tender love and kindness, looked down into the face of the little dirty, ragged boy and said, "My son, what church do you want to join?"

I said, "I don't know. How many have you?" I think he mentioned Baptists, Presbyterians, Christians and then the Methodists.

I said, "Which one of these are you a member of?" He replied, "I am a member of the Methodist church."

I said, "I want you to put me in the same church that you are in."

Then he said to me so kindly, "I will do that. How do you want to be baptized?"

I replied, "I don't know. When you baptize a fellow, how do you fix him up?"

He said, "Some people want to be immersed," and told me how that was done; "some people want to have the water sprinkled on them, but other people want to take the church vows and kneel down and have the water poured on their heads."

"Well," I said, "I want you to fix me up that way."

He said, "That's the way I'll baptize you." He sent for a little pitcher of spring water. It was the first glass pitcher that I had ever seen. Up to that time I did not know that you could make pitchers out of glass. I stood before him and he gave me the church vows. I will never forget when he said, "Dost thou renounce the devil and all of his works, the vain pomp and glory of the world, with all covetous desires? Will thou not follow or be led by them?" He instructed me how to correctly answer the questions.

I knelt down as he stood before me with the pitcher of water in his hand. I did not hear much of the ceremony but recall that he said, "My son, I baptize thee in the name of the Father, and of the Son, and of the Holy Ghost." By that time, the water was pouring down in a stream over my head. I began to shout as loud as I could, but he held me down and continued to pour the water over my head. When he finished, my head and shoulders were thoroughly wet. He had baptized boys with more sense than I possessed, but he never baptized one that made more noise and received more from a baptismal service.

Thank God for the fact that I had been converted, joined the church, taken the church vows and had been baptized. I was now on the road to heaven, in poverty, yet a millionaire; without a home, yet all heaven was mine. No doubt the reader has read the book, "Twice Born Men." I know what that means, for I was born the first time on the 27th day of January, 1860, in the mountains of Tennessee, but I was born the second time on the eleventh day of August, 1880, on the beautiful prairies of dear old Texas. Herein lies the difference between the two: I was born a rascal the first time, as one of the first recollections of my life was that of stealing something. I was born a Christian the second time and for more than forty-seven years I haven't taken a thing in the world that did not belong to me.

CHAPTER III

At the close of the campmeeting I went home and quit working on the ranch. I hired out to a man to dig stumps for fifty cents a day. I ate yellow cornbread and sorghum and drank warm tank water. About three months after my conversion I attended my first Sunday school. A young lady came around and asked me to join her class and I told her I desired to do so but could not. She wanted to know the reason why and I told her that I could not read. She said that made no difference as she would do the reading. So I joined and was enrolled in her Sunday school class. She read, I think, from John's Gospel and talked to us. She asked me if I had been converted and I said, yes. She looked me in the face and said, "When were you converted?" I undertook to tell her about the camp-meeting but just about that time God opened heaven and poured out such a flood of glory on my soul that I was shouting. A heavenly gale struck my soul and we shouted until we broke up the Sunday school. That was my first introduction to a Sunday school. Beloved, I wish I could be in one more Sunday school where they would break it up by shouting.

When the Sunday school was over, the young lady gave me a little testament. It was one of the first books I ever owned. I took it home and began to spell out the first chapter of Matthew. I found it hard spelling but said, "I am going to make a man out of Bud Robinson or die in the attempt." It wasn't long until I secured a pencil and said, "I will learn to write." The first copy book that I had was a barn door. I wrote on both sides of the barn door as high as I could reach. I tried to make the letters as I found them in the New Testament, so the reader can see at a glance that the copy book was not so bad. Then I found some large cardboards. I used my little testament as my copy book until I wrote on both sides of the boards. I was two or three days learning how to find Bud Robinson and writing it out on the cardboard. It was a long drawn out process but I said I was going to make a man out of Bud Robinson or die. I was making a start.

Then I began to attend church and tried to pray every time they called on me. About that time the call to preach came up before me and my, my, what burdens I had over my call to preach. I had no education, no money, and it looked like I had no friends. I was a bad stutterer and at that time fearfully afflicted. Of course the devil got busy and told me that I could never preach and I would agree with him. Then the devil would feel good and I would feel bad. I felt so miserable that I went to see an old Methodist steward. I tried to tell him that God had called me to preach and he said, "No, God never called a man to preach that had as little sense as you." He said that if I tried to preach I would disgrace the cause and bring reproach on the ministry, that it was all a mistaken idea of mine, and, said he, "Don't you ever try to preach."

My telling him that I would not seemed to relieve him somewhat but my burdens became so heavy that it looked like I was going to die.

I started back home and tried to tell the Lord that if He would find somebody else to preach I would help him all I could, but that I couldn't do it. By that time I was getting into darkness and it seemed like all the salvation in the world wouldn't get me to heaven if I did not preach. I finally went to see a man about it and as he talked worse to me than the other one, I left broken-hearted.

About that time a new preacher came on our. circuit. I went to hear him preach one Sunday morning and went home with him for dinner. After dinner, I took him down on the hillside below the little parsonage to tell him about my calling to the ministry, but I broke down and began to cry.

He said to me so kindly, "Brother Bud, I know what your trouble is. God has called you to preach and you don't think you can do it. Isn't that your trouble?" All I could do was to nod my head and he said, "I know what it means. I refused to preach until God had to nearly kill me and my family in order to get me into the ministry."

He said, "Brother Bud, God knows whom He wants to preach and if God wants you to preach, He will help you to do it. This afternoon I will put your name before the church and we will recommend you to the quarterly conference for license to exhort."

Well, glory to Jesus! That afternoon as he preached, I think I made more noise than he did. Once more my burdens were gone and the light of heaven was flooding my soul. I was getting back into God's purpose and plan for my life.

I want to say right here that a poor, ignorant boy has a hard time getting into the ministry because many of the best people seem to know that God did not call him to preach. If the poor fellow does not suit the folks, they do not think God called him. But the Lord sometimes calls people to preach that no one but the Lord would have called.

About two weeks from that time the presiding elder came around and I appeared before the quarterly conference. Never before was an examination conducted just like mine. That is, I have never heard of one like it. The good old elder asked me so kindly about history and of course I had never read one. He asked me about the English grammar and I had never seen one. He asked me about the discipline, and to his surprise, I didn't know that we had one. They talked a little bit and then sent me out. I must have been out for nearly an hour when they called me back and the presiding elder told me that they had granted me license to exhort. Later on I was told they kept me out so long on account of one young man making a speech against granting me license. He told them that I had no sense and if I was licensed to preach, I would never use it. Furthermore, my brothers were the worst men in the country, therefore he was convinced in his own mind that God had not called a man like me to preach.

After taking a vote they turned me down. But before they could proceed very far with the business, the Lord spoke to an old gentleman on the board who made a speech in which he said, "Brethren, we have done wrong in turning down this little boy. If God has called him to preach and we stand in his way, he may backslide and God may require his blood at our hands at the judgment. I move that we reconsider and grant this little boy license to exhort."

After reconsidering, they granted me the license which the elder wrote out. They were signed by the Rev. E. L. Armstrong, presiding elder of the Corsicana District of the Northwest Texas Conference of the Methodist Episcopal Church, South. I rolled up my license and put it in my breeches pocket and started for home, one of the happiest boys in the land. Ten years later the young man who voted and made a speech against me, came before my quarterly conference for license to exhort and I recommended him and shouted while the elder licensed him to exhort. You know the old country folks used to say that chickens come home to roost and surely it looked like it. He has long since gone to heaven for he was God's man.

About this time I went to work on a little farm for fifty cents a day, accumulated a small sum of money and rode about sixteen miles to the little town to buy my preacher's clothes. I bought three yards of checked cotton cloth that cost 12½c a yard to make a coat and three yards of the same kind of goods to make a pair of pants. So the reader will see that my coat and pants cost 75c. I bought three yards of speckled calico to make a Sunday shirt. Mother made my coat, pants and shirt which cost altogether 90c. I bought a 25c straw hat and paid $1.50 for a pair of brogan shoes, so coat, pants, shirt, hat and shoes cost the enormous sum of $2.65.

Up to that time I had received no calls to preach but I purchased a pony, tied on the old saddle with rawhide strings and put on cotton rope stirrups. I then had the little testament the little Sunday school teacher gave me and a little song book. In those days we did not wait for someone to call us. Therefore, one morning with Testament and song book in my pocket, I rode down to the settlement and galloped from ranch to ranch calling the people out and telling them that I was going to preach at the schoolhouse. I wanted them to come but stuttered so bad at times that I couldn't tell them what I wanted. They would laugh when I would stutter and tell them what I was going to do. They laughed long and loud, saying, "I'll be there."

Sure enough they came that night but what a struggle I had. I could sing two songs, "Jesus, Lover of My Soul," and "Amazing Grace, How Sweet the Sound." I stood up behind the little table with a little, old-fashioned brass kerosene oil lamp upon it. I sang one hymn and the big rough cattlemen with their spurs on looked at me as though I was crazy. After singing, I knelt down and tried to pray. I stuttered so I couldn't say a thing. The men all over the little schoolhouse were stamping on the floor and laughing. They were having a picnic at my expense but I finally choked it out and said Amen. I arose to my feet, and sang the other song. Nobody helped me and when the song was over, I began to preach. Opening my testament I read

a few verses, or tried to, at least. I think it must have
been from the Sermon on the Mount, yet I am not sure
for I was excited.

After I had read the verses I laid down my testament and undertook to say something. I began to
stutter until I could not say a thing. Those rough cattlemen began to laugh until it was pitiful. Finally,
when it looked like it would choke me down, God came
to my rescue. Instead of trying to preach, I broke
down and began to weep. The men quit laughing and
began to look serious. After crying awhile, God
changed the program. I quit crying and began to
shout. The glory came over me until it looked like I
was in heaven. I shouted as loud as I could whoop
and ran around the little table clapping my hands. By
that time the men began to look serious and after I had
shouted a while God changed the program on me and I
began to exhort. God took possession of me until I
was neither afraid of men nor devils. I walked up and
down the aisle of the little schoolhouse and exhorted
those men to flee from the wrath to come and get ready
to meet God. I told them that if they didn't repent of
their sins and get ready to meet God every man there
would be damned. That there was no power in the
known world that could keep them out of hell but the
mercy of God. That they must repent of their sins;
confess and forsake their sins; believe on the Lord
Jesus Christ and then God would help them to take
back everything they had ever stolen and help them to
make restitution and make their peace with God. They
seemed to believe God had come on the scene.

Then I began calling mourners. We did not have any mourner's bench but I had them kneel around the little table. Quite a number came and got down on their knees. I did not know how to conduct an altar service but I got down on my knees and began to scream as loud as I could and beat them on the back with my fists as hard as I could lay it on. Those rough cattlemen bawled like a yearling with a branding iron on him. Soon one of the men that I was beating on the back arose and told the folks that God had saved him. I went to another and began to beat him on the back and scream. Very soon he popped up and began to shout and yell and I crawled over to the next one and began to beat him and scream and soon he stood up. I don't know why I didn't say a word to the rest of the men who were on their knees. The three men and I had a tremendous time.

Finally I announced services for the next day at 11:00 o'clock and for the next night and then dismissed my congregation. The first man that was saved came and asked me to go home with him. We rode about six miles, arriving there about midnight. He asked me if I had been to supper. I said no, and no dinner either. He awoke his wife and told her he had religion and had brought the preacher home with him. He also told her to get me something to eat for I had had neither supper nor dinner. The good lady, who seemed to be in no hurry but rather embarrassed, finally brought out a pan of milk and a big breadpan full of cold biscuits. My, my! Cold sweet milk and cold biscuits at midnight! After I had galloped my pony all day, getting the people out, preached and shouted until midnight, I was hungry as a wolf and have never tasted anything better in my life. The good brother and I talked religion until one o'clock and attempted to get a little sleep. Next day he hitched the mules to his wagon and took his wife, children, and myself to the meeting.

The next day I did not try to preach much but I did have a great time crying, shouting and exhorting. I made an altar call and had several at the altar. The first to get saved was this man's wife. We had three saved during the morning service. By night the little schoolhouse was full and running over. Three were saved that night. During the first three services of my ministry, God gave me nine souls. The people wanted me to continue the meeting and no doubt I should have done so but I promised mother that I would come back on Monday, therefore I went home.

When the elder gave me the license to exhort, he said that we would have another quarterly conference in about three months, therefore wanted me to record every sermon I preached, the number of people saved and the number of homes in which I had preached and prayed. I would go out to preach and come home and tell my beautiful old Presbyterian mother what I had done. She would write it down for me. Up to the first quarterly conference, I had preached ninety times, exactly ninety people saved, and I had prayed in over two hundred homes. The report was almost as long as my arm, but as I could not read it correctly, the elder read it. He kindly said, "Brethren, this little boy has brought the best report I have ever known a licensed exhorter to bring in for one quarter. From the day we licensed him to exhort until this day, he has led one soul each day to Christ and is making a habit of preaching once each day." As a rule for the next six years, I preached every Saturday night and on Sundays. During the summer season I preached in three to four meetings.

CHAPTER IV

In 1886 Dr. W. B. Godbey held meetings across central Texas. He was called to hold a meeting at Alvarado, in Johnson County, Texas. I lived ten miles in the country and heard that there was a man in town preaching sanctification and that the people said he was crazy. They said he preached that a man could get so much religion that he would never get mad and didn't want to chew tobacco any more and that he couldn't sin if he wanted to. The people almost became wild. They said he was the craziest man on the subject of religion that they had ever heard of. I said, "I am going to hear him." So I saddled my pony and rode into Alvarado and heard him preach on entire sanctification as a second work of grace. After listening awhile I said, "That is the best religion I ever heard a man preach, but a man could not get it." About a week later I went back to hear him again and I said, "That is the best religion I ever heard a man preach in my life and it does look like one might get it." The reader can see that I was growing in grace.

After a few days my heart grew hungry and I went back to hear him the third time. I said, "That is the best religion that I ever heard a man preach and I will have it or die," so I became a seeker then and there for the experience of entire sanctification.

His meeting was far-reaching; people coming from

all parts of the country. He closed with a great convention. Rev. L. L. Pickett came all the way from Columbia, South Carolina, and Dr. Dunlap came from Atlanta, Georgia. Brother C. T. Hogan came from Ennis, Texas, with many other fine holiness people. That was my first introduction to a holiness meeting. It was during this convention that I heard Sister Mary Hogan, the wife of C. T. Hogan, preach. It was a great message. I believe that fifty to seventy-five people at the altar seeking God. For the next four years I did my best to get the experience.

Soon after the close of this convention, I moved from Johnson County to Hill County, Texas, but I went on with my work. After I had sought the blessing for two years, it seemed to me that if I would begin to preach holiness, I could get into the experience, therefore I began to preach holiness as a second work of grace. I told the people that I did not have it but that I wanted it worse than anything else. I recall that one preacher came to me and told me he did not believe in sanctification and he asked me if I had ever seen a preacher that had the blessing. I told him that I had seen a great many at the convention and that Dr. W. B. Godbey was the first man that I heard preach it.

I said to him, "Now Dr. Godbey has the experience."

He said, "How do you know that he has it?"

"Well," I said, "from the way he acted."

"How did he act?"

"Well," I said, "he did not act like anybody else. The men cussed him on the streets and he didn't talk back, and they broke stale eggs all over him and he didn't even wipe them off his clothes."

"Well," he said, "I would call a man like that crazy."

I said, "No, he was not crazy but sanctified." When he preached he did not even refer to the stale eggs. He preached and shouted and praised God just as though nothing had happened, and I said, "Finally the merchants felt ashamed of themselves and sent for him. They took him to a clothing house and gave him a new suit. They said it would disgrace the town to allow as great a man as Dr. Godbey to come to their city and be egged and cussed and leave with stale eggs on his clothes." They said they did not know what kind of religion he had but of its kind he had more of it and it was the best kind they had ever seen.

I preached holiness two years and that brought me down to the early summer of 1890. The first Sunday of June, 1890, in the morning I preached from 1 Thess. 5:23: "The very God of peace sanctify you wholly, and I pray God your whole spirit and soul and body be preserved blameless unto the coming of the Lord Jesus Christ." I preached the best that I could on holiness as a second work of grace and told the people that I didn't have it but that I wanted it and was going to have it at any cost. That night I preached about six miles from where I had preached in the morning, from Heb. 12:14: "Follow peace with all men, and holiness, without which no man shall see the Lord." God so burdened me that night for the experience that I wept as I preached and told the people that we were going to

have an altar service that night and we were going to
have at least one seeker and that was me. At the close
of my sermon I came down out of the pulpit and knelt
at the altar seeking the experience of holiness under
my own ministry. No sooner had I knelt than I heard
some man's big bootheels coming down the aisle, ker-
thump, ker-thump, ker-thump and he fell on his knees
at my side. It was F. M. McNary, our school teacher,
a Presbyterian elder, the most cultured and scholarly
gentleman in the community. He said, "Brother Bud,
you don't need this blessing any worse than I do," and
began to pray and ask God to sanctify Brother Bud.
While he prayed I said "Amen," for that was what I
wanted; to get sanctified wholly. When he said,
"Amen," then I began to pray for him. I prayed my
level best and he said, "Amen," and when I had finished my prayer we got up. Neither of us had got the
blessing, but we agreed as we shook hands that we
never would stop until God gave us that experience.

At the close of the service he said, "Go home with
me and let's talk it over." We got on our horses and
galloped across the prairies several miles to his home
and sat up and talked until one o'clock in the morning,
each telling the other what we thought it would do for
us when we got it. He brought out an old book written
years ago by the Presbyterians in which they had
called this experience "The Rest of Faith." He told
me that was the Presbyterian name for the experience
I was preaching. I told him the name the Methodists
gave it was "Sanctification or the Second Blessing
properly so-called." When one of the early Methodists

received this experience John Wesley said, "God did give you the second blessing properly so-called." The historians tell us that this was a new word John Wesley had coined; that the second blessing had never been heard of until he named it.

After we had talked until one o'clock in the morning, trying to make it plain to each other, we knelt and had prayer together and went to bed. At a very early hour I was up, had my pony saddled and rode home by the time my good mother was getting ready for breakfast. I unsaddled my pony and turned her into the big pasture, went to my room and hung up my saddlebags, and changed my clothing, getting ready for my day's work on the farm. When breakfast was over mother and I had prayer together and I went to the field and began to preach to Bud Robinson from the text I had used the night before: "Follow peace with all men, and holiness, without which no man shall see the Lord." I would pray awhile and thin corn awhile and then preach to Bud Robinson awhile. I did not get much corn thinned, though that was what I was supposed to be doing. My corn was up then beginning to tassle and silk, and I was pulling out the big weeds and taking out the corn where it was too thick. That was a good place to get sanctified, but beloved, the devil never allows any man to get the experience of sanctification without putting up a mighty fight. He fought me to the last ditch.

While I was thinning corn and preaching to Bud Robinson I could hear my brothers a few hundred yards away as they were plowing cotton. I could hear the rattle of their cultivators, the braying of the mules, and the boys driving the teams. But as long as I heard anything that was going on I did not get the blessing. I finally knelt and offered prayer. I tried to consecrate soul, spirit and body. I remember that I stood up and the last thing that I turned loose was my hoe handle. I saw everything I had: my farm, my mules, wagons and plows, and the crib of corn, the ricks of hay, and the pen of black hogs, and everything else floating off on the clouds.

I had begun to seek this blessing in 1886 and this was now the second day of June, 1890. There were four years that I had struggled trying to get perfect victory. I had often consecrated all that I had; I would put my mules, cows, hogs, corn and barn, and everything else on the altar and climb up on the pile and ask God to take us all, but that did not bring the victory. Beloved, the blessed old Book says, "Whatsoever touches the altar is made holy," and I had not touched the altar. There was a stack of hay, and a corn crib, and several big mules between me and the altar, but when I saw everything I had drift away and I was left alone with God in the cornfield it seemed to me I could hear the Lord say, "I will bring everything back and leave it here with you and I will go; or, if everything else goes then I will stay with you." I said, "Lord, let everything else go." Then I had that strange, peculiar feeling that God was so close to me that my soul trembled in God's presence and it seemed that God kindled up a fire in the very bottom of my heart.

The only way that I can describe the feeling is that anger boiled up, and God skimmed it off, and pride boiled up, and God skimmed it off, and jealousy boiled up and God skimmed it off, and envy boiled up and God skimmed it off, until it seemed to me that my heart was perfectly empty. I said, "Lord, there won't be anything left of me." God seemed to say, "There will not be much left, but what little there is will be clean."

When my heart was emptied, then it seemed that a river of peace broke loose in the clouds. It was as sweet as honey and the honeycomb. It flowed into my empty heart until a few minutes later my heart was full and overflowing and the waves of heaven became so great and grand and glorious that it seemed to me that I would die if God did not stay His hand. How little we know about the fullness of God and the greatness of God's power. Not half an hour before God cleansed me and filled me I had told the Lord that I wanted Him to come with all the power that He had and sanctify me. Then I had told the Lord that very morning that I had read in His Book that if I would bring all the tithes into the storehouse and prove Him He would open the windows of heaven and pour me out a blessing that there would not be room enough to receive it. Out of a hungry heart I had said, "O Lord, you cannot satisfy me with the windows of heaven; you will have to open the doors of heaven to pour out a blessing big enough to satisfy my hungry heart and soul;" but beloved, I did not know how large God's windows were and how small my heart was. God had never used that language but one time before and at that time God opened the windows of heaven and poured out a flood on the earth. If God's windows are so large that He can pour out a flood through them, then you can see at a glance that God's windows are large enough to pour out a blessing into the heart of one of His believing children to the extent that he cannot receive but little of it. As the waves of heaven rolled over my soul I finally got down on the ground and stretched out and as wave after wave of glory rolled over me, told the Lord that if He didn't hold up a bit there would be a dead man in the cornfield.

From that day to this I have been convinced that God can kill a man with His glory just as quick as He could kill him with lightning. On one occasion Moses said to the Lord, "Show me thy glory," and the Lord said, "You cannot see my face and live." That proves to me that to behold the glory of God would be to look upon His face and no man in the flesh could behold God's face and His glory and live. Therefore, in order to keep company with God, we will have to be glorified and this mortal will have to put on immortality.

After lying there in the field about three hours, for it was about nine o'clock in the morning when God sanctified me, it was about twelve when I got up and walked to the house. My beautiful old mother, who has been in heaven for a number of years, was an old-fashioned, shouting Presbyterian. She believed, "Once in grace always in grace," and she also believed that we could not be sanctified until we come to die, so for four years my precious old mother had argued with me that I would never get the blessing until I died. When

I walked up the hill and into the dining room my mother was putting dinner on the table. It was one of those old-fashioned country dinners cooked on the big wood stove. There was a big stove kettle nearly full of snap beans and streaked country bacon mixed with them; then mother had scraped two or three dozen new potatoes and laid them on the beans and as I went in and stood by the table my mother took up a large dish of beans and bacon and potatoes. I told mother that I had met Jesus Christ in the cornfield and He had sanctified my soul. My mother did not shout over the news of my being sanctified, bless her precious heart. She took up her checked apron and wiped a few trickling tears off her beautiful old face and went back to the stove and took out the big stovepan full of brown cornbread.

It might be interesting to the reader to know how these country mothers cooked cornbread in those days. My mother would go to the meal barrel and dip out a big sifter of cornmeal and sift the meal into the old-fashioned wooden breadtray, and then she would break two or three eggs, put in a spoonful of lard and about a spoonful of soda and a few cups of buttermilk and stir it up with a big spoon and pour it into the big breadpan and let it bake good and brown and when you cut it out in big squares about three inches square it would look almost like pound cake.

My mother took out the big breadpan, set it on the stove, got her knife and a big bread platter and cut out the bread in big square pieces till she had filled up the big platter. She came back and set it on the table.

Next she went and got a big two-gallon crock full of buttermilk and then brought on nearly a dozen pint cups for her boys and girls to drink milk out of. Now dinner was ready.

My mother looked sad. She would look out of the window and her chin would quiver and her eyes would fill up with tears. It looked to me like my mother thought that her preacher boy had lost his mind and would have to go to the insane asylum, for she had believed all the time that you never could get sanctified until you die and now I had got the blessing and behold I was wonderfully alive. But thank the Lord, after holding on in prayer and faith and believing God, and living the experience to the best of my ability, it wasn't many years until mother was gloriously and powerfully sanctified.

Beloved, it pays to get the blessing and to live it and preach it and sing it and shout it, for we have the best thing in the wide world, and why not let the world hear about it? The first man that I met after God sanctified me was one of the stewards of our church. I told him about my being sanctified in the cornfield. It seemed to insult him. He did not rejoice with me, but said with a vim in his voice that I will never forget, "Brother Bud, you had better go mighty slow about that sanctification business." He told me that it was nothing in the world but fanaticism, and wild fire and that if I didn't give it up I was ruined.

In a few weeks I started a meeting in the community and one of his boys who had been wild and reckless was beautifully saved in my arms. I had prayed many hours for the young man and God wondrously saved him, but his father then joined in with the Methodist circuit rider who was very bitterly opposed to holiness, and that dear father fought holiness until his boy backslid. That man lived to see the day when his son that he had caused to backslide was brought home from a night's carousal with a bullet through his body. His own father was the man that caused him to give up his experience and backslide.

Beloved, I have often said that a man had better fight a buzzsaw open-handed than to fight holiness. In a fight with a buzzsaw he might lose a hand or two, but to fight holiness he is liable to lose his precious immortal soul, and God has said, "What shall it profit a man if he shall gain the whole world and lose his own soul," and "What shall a man give in exchange for his soul?" It is remarkable what a price God puts on the soul. From what God says souls are a million times more valuable than worlds and see how little of this world any man will ever get. Many precious souls today are selling out entirely too cheap. A few years in sin, a dying struggle, an awful wail and a soul goes out to meet God.

Beloved, I thank God that for all of these thirty-seven years as a holiness preacher, though the preaching has been very poor, yet my heavenly Father and the devil know that I have been dead in earnest. I have never rounded off a corner, I have never called it by any name that I thought the rich, worldly people in the church would accept instead of the real experience, but I have called it entire sanctification; I have called it scriptural holiness; I have called it the second blessing; I have called it the baptism with the Holy Ghost and fire; I have told the people that the old man had to be crucified and that the body of sin had to be destroyed; that there was no such an experience as what has been called suppression; that there was not any such experience as counteraction.

We have found that regeneration is not an evolution but a revolution; regeneration is a revolution that turns a man upside down. Sanctification is not an evolution but a revolution; sanctification is a revolution that turns a man inside out, for we must be born of the Spirit before we could be baptized with the Spirit. Thank God, the new birth cleans a man up while the baptism of the Holy Ghost cleans him out. And if we are cleaned up and cleaned out, then we can be filled up and sent out, and there is no use to go if you don't go on fire for God.

If a preacher has no fire only what he carries in his pipe or on the end of his cigar, he may start a fire that will burn up the forest and burn down houses but he will never start a revival fire that will cause sinners to weep their way to the foot of the cross and find pardon. He cannot preach a gospel that will get justified believers wholly sanctified, for no man can preach beyond his experience. If he tries it, it will prove he is preaching beyond where he lives and it will have no weight with the people. God said, "Be ye clean that bear the vessels of the Lord." He also said that He made His angels ministering spirits and His ministers a flame of fire.

Thank God, since He put the fire in my soul I have scarcely been out of a good revival in thirty-seven years. I have seen them saved from ocean to ocean and from Canada to Key West, Florida; from the banks of the Pacific to the banks of the Atlantic. Thank God for a salvation from all sin for all men provided through the atoning blood of Jesus Christ. Today, as I dictate and hear the clicking of the keys of the typewriter as a young lady hammers off these words, my old heart is leaping for joy and I want to say, "Bless God, I am glad that I wasn't born a hundred years ago and died twenty-five years ago but I am glad that I was born in time to be alive now." I praise God that I was converted in time to get into the holiness movement and sanctified in time to get the movement into me. And today I am in the holiness movement moving the movement and the holiness movement is in me moving me. Glory to His name!

I think the first year after God sanctified me I had more people saved than I did during the ten years that I preached as a licensed exhorter and a licensed preacher without the experience of holiness, and yet I want to thank God that from the first time I preached God gave me souls. I have no idea what kind of a condition a preacher must be in and not be able to get people saved.

CHAPTER V

By 1891 I began to make plans to enter school at the Southwestern University. During the summer I held meetings and the people gave me some money to go to school on. One well-to-do widowed lady gave me fifty dollars. Up to that time that was the biggest sum of money that I had ever received in my life; for the first four years that I preached I received sixteen dollars. By the time I had preached ten years I had received about four hundred dollars, and the biggest part of that came in on the last year. By September I had gotten ready to leave the little farm in Hill County, Texas, and make a trip on the train to Georgetown, Texas, where the Southwestern University was located. This school was owned and operated by the Methodist Episcopal Church, South.

That, I think, was one of the greatest days of my life. I entered school on Tuesday, September 12, 1891. It was there that I met good men and great men who gave me a greater vision of life than I had ever had before. It was there that I began to read good papers and good books. Dr. John H. McClain was the president of the university and I judge that Texas never produced a finer character than Dr. John H. McClain. He had a great faculty, he himself taught in the university. His assistants were Prof. Colby, Professor Young, Professor Harris, Professor Sanders, Doctor

Moore, Professor Barcus, Professor Armstrong, Professor Kirkpatrick, and Professor Buckhead. These were as brilliant men as the Southern Methodist church could produce. The young ladies' annex was located at Georgetown, and Dr. John R. Allen was at the head of the young ladies' annex, with a fine band of teachers and many young ladies graduated from that school.

As I had had no previous schooling, I entered what was called the preparatory department and they called us boys "preps." Our teachers in the preparatory department were Professor Williams, Professor Barcus and Miss Lula Grant. At that time the Rev. Samuel P. Wright was the preacher in charge of the Methodist Church at the university and the Rev. Horace Bishop was presiding elder of the Georgetown district. There were two very fine literary societies in the university; one was called the Alamo and the other the San Jacinto. I joined the San Jacinto society and we had some very great debates in those societies. They were a great blessing to me from the fact that I learned how to think on my feet and to prove my points.

We had many fine young preachers in the college and of course as I was a young preacher I naturally fell in with the young preachers. While that has been many years ago, their faces and names linger with me yet. Some of our finest young preachers were John L. Brooks, E. M. Sweet, Ed Barcus, George and Tom Barcus, Frank S. Onderdonk, Rev. Jackson B. Cox, Rev. Ed Pilly. I remember that Brothers Onderdonk and Cox were preparing for the mission field in Old Mexico while Brother Pilly was preparing for China

and some of my roommates were very spiritual. There
was Rev. C. L. Brunner, J. J. Rape, R. J. Tooley,
Frank Mageehe and Brother George Hill. These young
men made a great impression on me. Our two literary
societies called some fine lecturers for each month during the school year. These men made a great impression on my heart and life. We had such men as Dr.
Briggs, the pastor of the First Methodist Episcopal
Church, South, of Austin, Texas. We had for one lecture Col. A. C. Bain from Lexington, Kentucky, one of
the finest lecturers I have ever heard. He was the
greatest prohibition lecturer of the nation. Also, they
had Rev. Samuel Small of Atlanta, Georgia.

Upon another occasion we had Gen. John A. Logan
of Tennessee, who was one of the most interesting men
on the great Civil War and the rising of the new South
from the old battle fields. We also had with us for one
lecture the famous Luther Benson, the reformed drunkard. He was the hardest hitter on the open saloon of
any man I have ever known. We had with us over one
Saturday and Sunday Bishop Joseph S. Key, at that
time one of the most spiritual men that I had ever
known. Upon another occasion we had Bishop Fitz-
gerald and his wife. He told us of the early days of his
experience in the great gold fields of California. He
was a very remarkable man. Upon another occasion
we had Dr. Rankin, a great Methodist preacher from
Houston, Texas, who a few years later was elected
editor of the Texas Christian Advocate.

I don't know but that almost every one of these
great lecturers has gone to his reward, but the impres-

sion they made on my life will go with me to my grave.
Good books and good papers and great men will be a
blessing to any man in the world. It was there in the
college that I began to read the Sunday School Times
and after such men as H. K. Trummel and Henry
Drummond, the man that wrote the little book on the
thirteenth chapter of First Corinthians and called it
the greatest thing in the world. Also, I read the Texas
Christian Advocate every week and many of the young
preachers took the National Advocate at the time that
Dr. Hoss was their editor. He wrote many great edi-
torials and a few years later was elected bishop.

At the closing of the school of 1892 I joined the
Rev. Horace Bishop, the presiding elder of the Georgetown district, and we worked on the district all summer
and finished up the campaign in the fall in time to go
to Waco to the annual conference. During that summer
we saw hundreds of people saved and we took people
into the Southern Methodist Church by the hundreds.
When we reached the annual conference I saw more
Methodist preachers and more presiding elders together than I had ever seen in my life. They were a
great class of men and there were some of the leading
men from the East Texas conference and the Texas
conference and the North Texas conference who were
there to visit the Northwest Texas conference. My
recollection is that Bishop Hargrove presided at this
conference but there is one thing that I will never forget that took place at that conference. There I met
the Salvation Army for the first time. I saw their uni-
forms, I heard their songs and shouts on the streets

and of course it almost blessed me to death to meet up with somebody that would hold street services.

By the time the conference was over I had found a place in the Salvation Army and straightway I ordered a uniform and a Salvation Army cap. I don't know now that I went in to stay with them very long but I wanted the experience of work that you could only receive by working on the streets and in the saloons and gambling houses and the slum district. As we worked in those places my very heart was stirred within me and I will never forget that in one month in Waco, Texas, we had sixteen little girls rescued from the slums and sent home to their mothers. We also had nearly twenty drunkards beautifully saved. Most of them were middle-aged men and some older who had been in what they commonly called the gutters most of their lives. We say now that they were down and out, but the Salvation Army used to say men are down but never out, and there may be something in that.

I stayed there in Waco and worked until Christmas. We had a general meeting of the officers of the state; there was a fine little officer from England named Thomas; they commonly called him little Zaccheus. He was at that time in charge of the state work and was an adjutant. In those days old Major Sulley was in charge of Missouri, Kansas, Texas and Oklahoma, which were all in his great division. L. Milton Williams, who now lives in Long Beach, California, one of our Nazarene elders, was at that time Major Williams. Brother Will Lee, who died a few years ago in Colorado Springs, at that time was known as Captain Lee.

Major Williams and Captain Lee were known as the Oklahoma devil drivers. I judge they had thousands of people saved. They neither feared men nor devils, hardship, abuse, empty purses and often retired at night with an empty stomach. They were as brave warriors as ever fought the devil on an Oklahoma battle field.

I worked in Waco under Captain Cooper and Cadet Dean. When I left Waco they sent me to Austin. I worked there with Captain Yeager and Cadet Doan. We had many experiences in those days that as a rule we know nothing about now. I have seen our soldiers knocked down by brickbats and on almost every hallelujah march somebody was either rocked, or egged, or they gave them a shower of rocks and rotten potatoes. Our free-will offerings were very large; they often consisted of dead cats, brick-bats, stale eggs and mud balls. But God was with the Army and people were saved by the hundreds and thousands. I have seen them in the street meetings preach to such crowds that the streets were blocked. I have seen the officers come and open the way and many a Salvation Army boy received an awful cussing from the police. Other times they were arrested and locked in jail, but they prayed and shouted so loud that nobody in jail could sleep and next day they would turn them out. By seven-thirty at night you could hear the Salvation drum, the old bugle and the lads and lassies were out on another Hallelujah march.

One night while we were standing on the corner of Third and Main Streets, Austin, Texas, just below the

state house, singing a song, somebody threw a brick-bat
into the crowd and struck one of our young men on the
head and cut a gash two inches long just above his ear.
The dear boy fell like he had been shot. Two of the
boys went up to the hall and got a stretcher and we
carried him to the hall and it was thirty minutes before
he knew what had happened. As we washed the blood
from his head and face he said, "God bless the poor
sinner and save his soul." Beloved, it takes lots of
grace for a man to be stoned and half killed and then
pray for his enemies. But the Salvation Army boys
and lassies thirty-five and forty years ago had that
much grace.

One of the most remarkable experiences of my life
took place while we were in the Salvation Army at
Austin. Our offerings had been very small and after
meeting the hall rent and expenses for the month we
had but little left for food. At one time we lived three
weeks on bread and tea, and no sugar for the tea. The
bread was that old, early-day bread that was so tough
when you bit it your teeth would nearly pop, and I got
so hungry that often as I went marching down the
street beating the drum, at the head of my soldiers,
going by a restaurant and smelling the beefsteak fry-
ing, my stomach would growl like a dog under the floor.
But I had to say, "Lie down, I haven't got anything for
you."

In those days we often prayed four hours a day
from house to house. I entered a beautiful little cottage
home, set some fifty feet back from the street. A nice-
looking little lady was running a sewing machine while

two or three little tots were playing on the floor. I told her that I had come to have prayer with her and the little ones.

"Sir," she said, "you cannot pray in this house."

I said to her kindly, "You may run your machine and just let me kneel and pray here alone for you and the little ones."

She said, "No sir, you cannot pray in this house."

"Well then," I said, "will you let me pray out in the yard?"

She said, "No sir, you cannot pray in this yard."

Then I said, "Will you let me pray out on the sidewalk?"

She said, "That is just with you about that."

So I went out on the sidewalk and took off my cap and sang a good Salvation Army song and knelt and prayed on the sidewalk. I don't know, but it seemed to me that I couldn't hear the machine while I was praying. I believe she quit sewing and listened. When the prayer was over I went on up the street. That night we had a good time on our hallelujah march and in the hall, with a number of precious souls saved. The next day in making our rounds praying from house to house the blessed Holy Ghost said, "Go back by that house and see if the lady will let you pray with her." So I went back to the home as though I had never been there before. The little lady was running the machine. I told her that I had come around to have prayer with her if she had no objection. In somewhat of an embarrassed manner she pushed back from the machine and apologized for what she had said the day before. I fixed it up for her the best I could.

I said, "I know you were very busy yesterday and had no time to be bothered."

Then she said, "What kind of people are you?"

"Well," I said, "we are just religious people. But we are called the Salvation Army."

"Well," she said, "I don't know anything about the Salvation Army."

She took one of the babies in her lap and I took out my testament and read and then we knelt and prayed. The Lord melted my heart to tears and I asked God to bless the little lady and all of her loved ones.

When the prayer was over I said, "I want you to come down to the hall and enjoy our good meetings." I told her where the hall was located. She said she didn't know whether she could come or not but she would try. Some way I felt God was going to send her. That night after we ate our scanty supper of weak tea and tough bread without meat or potatoes or eggs, feeling hungry and weak, we went out on our march. A fine street service was held and when we got back to the hall, behold, the little lady was on the front seat. We gave her a hearty welcome to our meeting. The Lord helped me to preach that night and when I made the call she was the first to come out to the penitent form and before the close of the service she was most gloriously saved.

She said to us, "My husband is a railroad conductor and he gets in tonight about midnight and doesn't have to go out tomorrow until after twelve. If you can all come I would be so glad to get you a good chicken dinner tomorrow. Do you think you could arrange to come?"

I said, "Yes, ma'am, I think we could."

"Well," she said, "I want you to come a little early so we can have dinner by eleven so my husband will have time to get acquainted and eat dinner before he goes on his run."

I said, "We will be there, God sparing us."

That was the best news we had heard for a long time. The next morning we were up and studied and prayed and by ten o'clock we were pulling toward that cottage home.

My, my, but that was a great chicken dinner. It lingers with me yet. Reader, just think of it; three weeks of tough bread and weak tea and now a baked hen and dressing piled up before us. Her husband was a most congenial gentleman. He seemed to be delighted to have the Salvation Army boys visit his home but it was some two or three weeks before his run was changed so he could be with us for a night, but one night he and she walked in together with their babies. He was most gloriously saved that night. I never will forget that fine old conductor as he stood up with tears running down his face and thanked God that the Salvation Army had come to their home. That good man and his wife proved to be the best friends we have in Austin, Texas. Suppose that when the lady would not allow me to pray in her house or yard, I had showed an ugly spirit and hadn't prayed on the sidewalk and sung and gone back the next day. We never would have gotten those people saved. Think of what I had to do in order to get a square meal. I had to make two trips to that home and get a woman saved. I remember we used to sing the little song,

"It pays to serve Jesus, for I speak from my heart.
 He'll always be with us if we'll do our part,
 There is nought in this wide world such pleasure affords,
 As the peace and joy that comes from serving the Lord."

I remember another beautiful tune that they used to sing. In those days there was a song written and scattered over the land called, "After the Ball." The Salvation Army got hold of the tune and put their own words to it. I remember the church people called it a bad tune but the Salvation Army said all tunes were good tunes except one, the spittoon. The Army said God owned all the tunes and the devil owned the spittoons. One verse was,

"I saw the world in sinfulness lie
 Cursed by the law and condemned to die.
 No eye to pity, no arm to save,
 I came to conquer death and the grave.

"Bearing the cross of Jesus, stooping to save the lost,
 Ready to save the lowly, willing to pay the cost.
 Bearing the reproach of Jesus, faithful through sin's dark
        night;
 Jesus will crown with glory, after the fight."

Many a night I have heard the streets sound with the Salvation Army singing those beautiful words to the tune of "After the Ball."

CHAPTER VI

The first of January, 1893, I gave up Army work, as it was hard on my lungs and voice to sing so much in the open air, and went up to Georgetown where I had two years before been in school. By this time I had become engaged to Miss Sally Harper and on January 10, 1893, we were united in holy wedlock. That was another epoch-making day in the history of my life. Two years later the Lord sent little Sally to bless our home. This was our first-born child and of course it was natural that I should name her for her mother. After all these years she is still to us little Sally, though at this writing she is married and has seven sweet, beautiful children. Three years after little Sally was given us the Lord sent little Ruby to bless our home. And while she is our baby and in a sense as little and sweet as she used to be, she is also grown and married, but lives with her mother and father. Little Sally married the Rev. W. A. Welch, a fine sanctified young preacher. Ruby girl married the Rev. George C. Wise, also a fine sanctified young man and called to preach and sing the gospel.

In 1898 we left Georgetown, Texas, and I organized and worked on the Hubbard Circuit of Hill County, Texas. At that time, I had united with the Methodist Episcopal Church. The Hubbard Circuit was in the Fort Worth District and in the Austin Annual Confer-

ence and Rev. R. L. Selle was my presiding elder.
After two years we changed elders and then the Rev.
T. H. Corkel was my elder until I left the Hubbard
Circuit on the last day of August, 1900. In 1899 we
had established the Texas Holiness University at
Greenville, Texas. I was called to Greenville to hold
the spring session of the Greenville campmeeting, which
always meets now in August; but this spring session
met in May. In May, 1899, during the convention the
school board that we had gotten together called Rev.
A. M. Hills to take charge of the new school. He arrived in Greenville during this meeting. The plans
were all laid to establish a school to open the September
following.

I went back on the circuit and worked until the last
of July and then went to North Texas and held one
campmeeting at the Bates camp ground and one at the
camp ground at Denton, Texas, and then went to
Greenville for their campmeeting in August. We had
bought a lot on the school ground. We went to Hubbard again and packed up our things and shipped them
to Greenville and left the Hubbard Circuit on the last
day of August, 1900, and moved to Greenville and located on the school ground. During the fall and winter
of 1900 I evangelized, going as far north as Chicago
and as far south as Indiana, Kentucky, Tennessee and
Arkansas. During 1901 I had a full slate and did more
traveling than I had ever done up to that time, traveling more than 20,000 miles.

When the spring of 1902 rolled around Rev. Will
H. Huff, of national and world-wide fame, joined me

and we made up the Huff and Robinson Evangelistic
Party and traveled together for six years. Brother Huff
had gone to Asbury College at Wilmore, Kentucky, in
1898 and studied a year under Dr. A. M. Hills. He
was so well pleased with Dr. Hills that he came to
Texas with him in 1899 and studied under the Doctor
for 1898, 1899, 1900, 1901 and until the last of May,
1902. He says that Dr. Hills is the greatest teacher
that the holiness movement has ever produced.

Our first trip after Brother Huff and I united, my
wife and Brother Huff and myself left Greenville in
May and made a trip to Sioux City, Iowa. Brother
Huff was a stranger to the people there. I had done
some work through Iowa in 1901 with Mrs. M. J.
Tylor, the president of the Woodbury County Holiness
Association. Mrs. Tylor called me for her May meeting that was to be held on the grounds of Morningside,
a suburb of Sioux City near the Morningside College.
In this meeting Miss Metta Tylor, the youngest daughter of Mrs. Tylor, was beautifully sanctified. She later
became Mrs. Will H. Huff. From Sioux City we went
to Denison, Iowa, to a very great campmeeting. The
called workers for that camp were Rev. Seth C. Rees,
Rev. Andy Dolbow, Bud Robinson and Will Huff.
Rev. Thomas A. Teas was the song leader.

From Denison, Iowa, we went to the great Rocky
mountains, spending a day in Colorado Springs, taking
in the Garden of the Gods, Glenaria, Manitou Springs,
the Seven Falls and climbing the bluffs to see Helen
Hunt Jackson's grave. Our first meeting there was in
Pueblo, Colorado. There the Lord gave us a very

great revival. We worked there with Rev. Kent White.

We went then to Cripple Creek. I have before me a beautiful letter from J. N. Tomlin. He says that the convention in Cripple Creek and Victor was from June 16 to 19, and that Brother Tomlin and wife were in charge of the work at Cripple Creek while Miss Leak was in charge at Victor. In those days Cripple Creek, Victor and Bull's Hill were the gold fields of Colorado. Brother and Sister Tomlin and Miss Leak were at that time working under Mrs. Kent White with her head-quarters on Champa street in the city of Denver.

Brother Tomlin writes, "You were a great blessing to me and my wife and the blessing remains with me until today. At this writing and for the past four years I have been with the Church of the Nazarene." He writes me this note from Haxton, Colorado, where he is pastor of the church. May the Lord bless Brother and Sister Tomlin.

When we left Cripple Creek we stopped again for a day or two in Colorado Springs and it was arranged for me to preach in one of the Baptist churches. There I met the Rev. I. G. Martin for the first time, and for all of these years we have been the warmest of friends. While we preached in the First Baptist church he and Brother William Lee had called Rev. L. Milton Williams to hold a big meeting in Colorado Springs and there we heard Brother Williams for the first time. This was in June, 1902. Since then the Lord has allowed me to fight many battles with these two warriors. Martin and Williams have been great soldiers and have fought the devil from ocean to ocean and from the Lakes to the Gulf.

From Colorado Springs we ran over to Denver and held a meeting for Mrs. Alma White. Had nearly two weeks in Denver. This brought us down to the middle of July. At that time Miss Emma Baller had arranged a campmeeting at Kensington, Kansas, and had called Brother Huff and me to be the preachers, so we went from Denver to Kensington. We had a good meeting and went from Kensington to our home in Peniel, Texas. This brought us to the first of August, 1902.

After a few days' rest we went to a big campmeeting at Marthasville, Louisiana. At that time I was almost killed by the mosquitoes and had a congestive chill and I suspect I would have died if it had not been for the prayers of Brother Huff and Sister William Matthews from Peniel, Texas. One got on each side of the bed and prayed me back to life. Then we went back to Arkansas and held a campmeeting in Beebe.

We went back to my Peniel home and Sister Robinson, Brother Huff and I left Peniel, Texas, the last of September, making our way East to join Dr. Fowler in the city of Boston on the third day of November, to make a coast-to-coast campaign. We stopped and preached in Evansville, Indiana. From there to Tipton, Indiana, and preached for the dear old boys in their annual conference of the Holiness Christian Church. Had a glorious time with these boys.

We went from there to Indianapolis and had a great meeting in the holiness tabernacle with Dr. Bye, Brother Fergerson, Andy Dolbow and precious old Father

Haney. At this writing Father Haney and Ed Fergerson both have gone to live with Jesus. Our meeting
was a wonderful revival.

Leaving Indianapolis we stopped a few days in East
Liverpool, Ohio, and stayed a few days with Brother
Huff's brother, Elmer, who a few years ago went up to
live with Jesus. Our next stop was in the First Methodist church in Washington, Pennsylvania. God gave
us a great revival in that church. They had a fine
pastor. He and his good wife and two sisters were
gloriously sanctified in the meeting and more than fifty
members of his church. We stopped two days in Washington, D. C., sight-seeing in the city. We stopped a
couple of days in New York City to behold the wonders, and on Friday morning, November 3, 1902, we
pulled into Boston. The convention opened that night
at the Bromfield Street church. Here we had a great
convention. It was simply marvelous what God did.
In this convention Dr. E. F. Walker was with us for
three or four great services. The music was in charge
of J. M. and M. J. Harris, at that time the greatest
gospel singers in the United States.

At the close of the Boston convention as we had
more work than we had time to give, we divided the
party, Dr. Fowler and his wife, Dr. E. F. Walker and
J. M. and M. J. Harris going to Providence, R. I., for
a great convention and Dr. Fowler sent Will Huff, my
wife and me to Haverhill, Mass., to hold a convention
in the holiness church of which the Rev. Isaac Hanson
was pastor. We ran there over ten days and this was a

very great convention. I was there one night last October and met people who were sanctified in the convention of November, 1902.

At the close of the Haverhill convention our little party boarded the train and were headed for Jamaica, Long Island, down in New York state. When we reached Providence, R. I., Brother and Sister Fowler, Dr. Walker and Brother and Sister Harris boarded the train.

We went to New York and transferred across to Jamaica. The convention was held there in a large Methodist church. Dr. Burns was the pastor. He was one of the finest Methodist preachers, the most loving, gentle, kind, sweet-spirited man that I think I had ever met up to that time. He wrote my wife and me after that several times a year until he went to heaven. Our convention there was a very great convention. There were many fine holiness preachers at that time known as the Association of Pentecostal Churches in New England. I remember Brother William Howard Hoople of Brooklyn, New York, was with us during this convention. He was one of the great men that later on brought the Association of Pentecostal Churches into the Church of the Nazarene. Brother Hoople was one of the leaders of that great movement; in fact, he was the founder of the Pentecostal Church.

From Jamaica we made our way to Reading, Pennsylvania. Here God gave us a great convention. From Reading, Pennsylvania, we made a trip to Cincinnati, Ohio. There I visited for the first time God's Bible

School. Our convention in the city was owned of the Lord. At the close of this convention Brother Fowler went to Chicago for a few days of business just before the holidays, and sent Brother Huff and wife and me to Troy, Ohio, to a holiness convention that was held by Brother and Sister Warner. At the close of our convention we joined our party in Cleveland, Ohio, and had one of the greatest meetings I had ever seen up to that time, with Brother and Sister Malone in the Friends Bible College on Cedar avenue.

Our trip from Boston to Los Angeles took over six months' travel and in the Friends Bible School we received the largest offering on this entire trip. There was one little wad of bills rolled up and tied hard in a little knot. When they were straightened out and counted there was more than three hundred dollars in that little bundle. No finer people ever lived than Brother and Sister Malone, but bless her memory, she has gone to glory.

Our next convention was in Chicago. This was a very remarkable convention. People came by the multiplied hundreds, the altars were lined day and night. Our next stop was in the St. James church in the city of Denver. Our good Brother Allen, who has long since gone to heaven, was pastor there. From Denver we went to Colorado Springs. Our convention was owned of the Lord. When we closed in the Springs, we came back to Denver and spent the night and left Denver on the first day of March, 1903, headed for California.

That trip was one never to be forgotten. I remember that Brother S. B. Rhodes and wife and some from Colorado Springs went with us to Denver and we almost filled up one Pullman car from Denver to Sacramento. We had in our party Dr. C. J. Fowler and wife, J. M. and M. J. Harris, Brother Jim Harris, the brother of John, Brother Will Huff, S. B. Rhodes and wife and son, Bud Robinson and Miss Sally. Our trains did not make as good time as they make now and we were several days coming from Denver to Sacramento.

Our convention there was held in Peniel Hall, which was run by Brother and Sister Ferguson in those days. It may be that some readers of this book remember Brother and Sister Ferguson had a string of missions from Southern California to Alaska and other parts of the world. There are still at this writing a few of these missions in operation. From Sacramento we ran to San Francisco. We were there over two Sundays and had a very great convention. I will never forget one afternoon that Dr. Fowler was preaching a fine-looking woman, handsomely gowned, well loaded with jewelry, sat on the front seat, just as drunk as she could be. While he was preaching she would look up and say, "The Lord pity the poor old devil." It was so embarrassing to Dr. Fowler that he could scarcely preach. After a while she went to sleep and fell off of the bench and that was too much for the dear old doctor. I got up and said, "Doctor, sit down and let me have this service." The great, good man turned around and said, "Brother Bud, you can have it." If ever the Lord helped me to preach and shout He did that afternoon. We knelt all around the drunk woman and God saved her.

While we were in Sacramento and San Francisco Rev. C. E. Cornell from Cleveland, Ohio, one of our greatest and best evangelists in those days, had come to Los Angeles to hold a meeting for Dr. P. F. Bresee, the founder and organizer of the first Church of the Nazarene in the United States; or, as far as we know, in the world. We closed our convention in San Francisco the second of April and on that day in Los Angeles the great Nazarene church on the corner of Sixth and Wall streets had just been completed. That noble band of Nazarenes marched from the old tabernacle on Los Angeles street to their great church home on the corner of Sixth and Wall. In one offering they laid on the table that day more than ten thousand dollars in cash.

We left Frisco on Monday after the first Sunday in April and landed in Los Angeles on Tuesday. Here we were met at the depot by Dr. Bresee and Brother Cornell and a great band of the Nazarenes. Our great convention opened on Tuesday night. But here is one point I must not forget: A year before Rev. C. W. Ruth, of Indianapolis, had come out to Los Angeles as Dr. Bresee's assistant and stayed until after Christmas, 1903. We met him in Denver in the St. James Methodist church and that was the first time I had ever met Brother Ruth. He preached for us one afternoon and brought us a great message from the third chapter of Matthew, on John and Jesus as the two baptizers, water representing the new birth and the Holy Ghost and fire representing sanctification. By the time we came out and held the conventions in Sacramento and Frisco, Brother Ruth had come from the East and joined with us in the great convention at Los Angeles. It was in this meeting in the First church where I met for the first time Rev. Joseph Jemerson, a great Irishman, born across the mighty deep. I believe he was one of the greatest orators at that time on the American continent. I will never forget some of the prayers that man prayed. I have known him to pray until men and women would rise up on their knees in the congregation and look at him.

Our convention was one that I will never forget. On Sunday morning, Rev. J. P. Coleman, who had united with the Church of the Nazarene from another denomination, stood on the great platform and read one of the Psalms. It was the most beautiful I had ever heard. How wonderfully God does things. At this writing as my home is in beautiful Pasadena, after twenty-three years of wandering up and down the land, behold Brother Coleman and I live just one block apart and he visits my home almost every day. At the close of our great revival in the Nazarene church I had a few services in the Peniel Hall in Los Angeles for Sister Ferguson. Then my wife and I went out to East Los Angeles and held a meeting in a little Southern Methodist church for a young Brother Fisher, a fine young man. At that time Brother and Sister J. M. and M. J. Harris and Will Huff and Jim Harris all took off a month for rest and went to Catalina island. Our trip over there was very interesting. I had never seen people seasick before. Among others who went over was Brother C. W. Ruth. He got so sick that he lay down on the boat and when asked what he wanted, he said he wanted his mother. I remember Will H. Huff became almost as limber as a rag and about as pale as a corpse, dark green circles came around his eyes and he got down on the floor and called for a bucket. But it was a wonderful day.

While our good friends were resting on the island my wife and I made our way back to Colorado Springs. There we rested up for a month with the exception that I preached every Sunday morning and night for Brother Will Lee in the People's Mission. We roomed in their home. When we left California we had written to my wife's niece, Miss Maggie Price, who lived with us and kept house for us in Peniel, Texas, and took care of our girls, little Sally and Ruby girl, while we traveled. We sent for them and they joined us in Colorado Springs. We had a full month together. We went out almost every day to see the great springs and mountains and canyons. We visited the Garden of the Gods and Williams canyon and South Cheyenne canyon and North Cheyenne canyon and the beautiful Manitou Springs, the Seven Falls; also we took our girls to Helen Hunt Jackson's grave. This lady was a very great novelist and wrote her novels up above these great falls. When she died she requested to be buried up there.

Our stay in the home of Brother and Sister Lee is one that will linger for many years. Our precious Brother Lee has been translated since then. We stayed with him over the last Sunday of May and ran down to the city of Denver and had a three days' convention for the National Holiness Association. From there we went to the National Holiness Campmeeting at Des Moines, Iowa. Dr. Fowler was in charge of this great camp and Brother Huff and J. M. and M. J. Harris joined us at Des Moines. There we had a great campmeeting. I remember a great man that came from Missouri, J. M. O'Brien, and he brought with him a number of young preachers on purpose to get them sanctified. One young man I remember very distinctly was Rev. C. F. Wimberly. From that day to this Brother Wimberley has been one of the outstanding writers and second blessing holiness men of the South. He later on went to Louisville, Kentucky, and entered the office of the Pentecostal Herald and worked for Dr. Morrison for many years.

At the close of this camp Dr. Fowler hired Rev. Will H. Huff and myself for the entire summer. We had meetings in such cities as East Liverpool and established the great campmeeting at Sebring, Ohio, which has become of national fame. We also preached in such camps as Findlay, Ohio, Portage and Hollow Rock. These camps are well known to the readers of the various holiness journals.

In finishing up our summer's campaign, working through September and October we again went to Boston and joined Dr. Fowler and made another national coast-to-coast campaign. We made almost the same run as the year before. We were in Boston, Haverhill, Providence, Rhode Island; Jamaica, Long Island; Cleveland, Ohio; Youngstown, Ohio; Chicago, Illinois; and Denver, Colorado, in the St. James Methodist church with our beloved Brother Allen, that we referred to in our first campaign across the country. Brother Allen is now walking the golden streets of the New Jerusalem. He was one real walking saint.

CHAPTER VII

When we finished up in Denver we all took a short rest before we were to meet again at Los Angeles. When we were there in 1903 Dr. Bresee engaged Dr. Fowler, Dr. H. C. Morrison, J. M. and M. J. Harris and this writer to give him the month of May, 1904. At the close of my convention in Denver I ran down to Texas and while I rested I ran over to Birmingham, Alabama, and held a convention and from there went across the country to McAlester, Oklahoma, and closed a meeting there the last Sunday of April, 1904.

In that convention Brother C. K. Spell joined me. He went home with me and we left Peniel, Texas, headed for Los Angeles, California, on the last Tuesday of April, 1904. Brother C. K. Spell made the statement that he was going to Los Angeles and take in the general conference which was to be held in the month of May, 1904. He said in taking in the conference he would get some sense. He said he was going then to San Francisco and attend a great conference by Dr. B. Carradine and there he said he would get him some religion. Then he had planned to go to Salt Lake City, and said, "There I will be sure to get me a wife," and sure enough, before he had finished the convention in Salt Lake City he had fallen in love with Miss Annie Price, who later became his wife. There is some history that I helped to make for I arranged this slate for Brother Spell.

Our convention with Dr. Bresee for the month of May, 1904, was one of the greatest I have ever worked in. As I have just stated, the general conference of the Methodist Episcopal Church was in session in Dr. Bresee's tabernacle. We had services in the afternoon and night and that gave us a chance to visit the general conference every morning. I will never forget some of the great debates between Dr. J. M. Buckley, editor of the New York Christian Advocate, and Dr. B. F. Neeley, who was elected bishop at that conference. I think there was scarcely a morning for a month that those great men didn't cross swords on some question. They were both men of master minds and great thinkers. There were a number of great men elected bishops in that conference: Dr. Neeley, Dr. Berts from Rome and Rev. Joseph Berry, editor of the Epworth Era. Dr. Berry was elected on the first ballot. Also Dr. Lewis was elected bishop, who was at that time president of the Morningside College, a suburb of Sioux City, Iowa. I think Dr. Day of Syracuse, New York, was elected bishop but he refused to be consecrated.

We had in the great Nazarene tabernacle more than five hundred people saved. After we had run there for a week or two, it was arranged that every afternoon when the general conference adjourned Bishops Joyce, Mallalieu and McCabe put on what is known as the pentecostal services, held every afternoon at four o'clock at the great Baptist temple and then Dr. Bresee arranged for our regular afternoon services from two to four so we could go to the pentecostal services. Rev. Joseph H. Smith was appointed to do the most of the preaching, but they called on Dr. Morrison to preach a number of times. Bishop Joyce arranged one afternoon for Dr. P. F. Bresee, pastor of First Church of the Nazarene, to bring a message to the great multitude of perhaps three thousand people and J. M. and M. J. Harris were called on to do a good deal of singing at that pentecostal rally. One afternoon, without consulting me, which was very exciting, Bishop Joyce called me from the congregation to come to the platform and to quote for the people the Fifty-fifth chapter of Isaiah's prophecy. The dear old bishop pulled his handkerchief and wiped the tears off his eyes and said, "Thank God, that there is a man who can read the Bible without looking at it."

About that time an old Methodist preacher from the Puget Sound conference, Rev. John Flynn, who was then eighty-eight years old, got up and began to leap in the air and praise God with a loud voice. Bishop McCabe jumped up and said, "People, people, people, listen to me! Take one good look at that man. He is eighty-eight years old and he won't superannuate. As you look at him just remember that the devil has no happy old men." It was the first time I had heard that expression and it stayed with me like burrs in the sheep's wool. While dear Brother Flynn was leaping and shouting his dear old wife jumped up and said, "Friends, I am feeling just like John is acting," and the shouts of the people broke up the meeting. When the shouting subsided Bishop Joyce called for Brother and

Sister Harris to come forward and sing that old hymn, "The Old Fountain." Before they finished it I believe a thousand people were waving handkerchiefs and hands. Bishop Joyce said, "Beloved, beloved, this is a pentecostal meeting and God is able to send pentecostal waves of glory today as He did in olden times." Those were days that I will never forget.

Before leaving this I might recall one incident that was very interesting. On the last Saturday of April, before opening our great convention, Dr. Bresee, Dr. Morrison, J. M. and M. J. Harris, C. K. Spell and Bud Robinson, with a number of others, made our way to Long Beach, California, and secured a fine fishing boat. That is, we all paid the man and his son to take us as far as eight miles out on the ocean for deep water fishing. They furnished all the fishing tackle and we got all we caught. There were probably twenty-five or thirty in the party. As we went on with our trolls out about four miles in the ocean we ran through a school of the big fish called yellowtails. The fish looked almost like a big river trout but the big fans on their tails were as yellow as gold. They were simply beautiful. We caught four at the same time. Within ten seconds of each other our lines were pulled under and all hands began to whoop and yell and scream. Sister Harris shouted, "I caught the first one," and I think her hook was pulled under first. It was so near the same time we caught the four that you could scarcely tell who caught the first but we gave Sister Margaret credit for catching the first. I think Dr. Morrison's hook and mine went down at the same moment. Dr.

Morrison stood up and waved his hat and shouted while the man and his son that ran the boat pulled in our hooks. No boy ever had a greater time than Dr. Morrison on that fishing trip. These four fish weighed about seventy pounds. They weighed seventeen or eighteen pounds each. Our whole party caught several hundred pounds. I remember in the afternoon I caught a big, long, round fish that they called a barracuda. He only weighed four or five pounds but he was between four and five feet long and was very interesting and fine eating.

I brought mine to Los Angeles and took them to a good friend of mine, Brother Clyde T. Dilley, who a year before had come from Waco, Texas, and located in Los Angeles. It was during this great convention that Dr. Bresee took Brother and Sister Dilley into the Church of the Nazarene. At that time I belonged to the Methodist Episcopal church and did not unite with the Church of the Nazarene until the sixth of April, 1908. Of course I was on the log for some four or five years and finally the Holy Spirit pushed me off the log and I fell into the Church of the Nazarene. We'll see about that a little later on.

At the close of this great convention, which was the last Sunday of May, Dr. and Sister C. J. Fowler, J. M. and M. J. Harris and this writer left Los Angeles for the Des Moines, Iowa, camp. We made the trip by El Paso, Kansas City, Missouri, and on across to Des Moines. This also was a great convention. At the close of that convention I worked again for Dr. Fowler until fall. But I did not join in their coast-to-coast campaign again until a number of years later.

From that on to 1908 Brother Will Huff and I preached as far north as Washington and Oregon, North and South Dakota, Minnesota, as far east as Old Orchard, Maine, and as far down in the southeast as Key West, Florida. We held a number of great meetings in Florida. We went four years in succession to Bennettsville, South Carolina. One year I. G. Martin went with us and had charge of the music and then Brother Charles J. Tillman stayed at least three years with us. Brother John Langrom, the blind boy, presided at the piano and Brother Bowen Grandfield, at that time just from Wales, was one of the finest flute and piccolo players I had ever heard. At one time he was a member of King Edward's band in England. He was with us nearly every year after that. He and I held meetings in a number of places in the South. In some of our meetings, Brother C. P. Currie led the singing. He is now one of the leading Southern Methodist preachers of Oklahoma. At Bennettsville we met for the first time that great old southern warrior, Brother Jim Williams, at one time a great blacksmith. He got saved and sanctified and went into evangelistic work. He wore out not less than fifteen good gospel tents in North and South Carolina and Georgia. He was a very remarkable man.

In one of our great campaigns in Bennettsville a young man by the name of Baxton McLendon, who at the present time is known as "Cyclone Mac," was gloriously and powerfully saved. Today Cyclone Mac is by far the greatest preacher in the Southland. Before his conversion he was one of the wildest, wickedest and most desperate and dangerous men in South Carolina. I prayed seventeen days and nights for Baxton Mc-Lendon. I will never forget the first night he came under the big tent. He sat near the back, his black eyes fairly glittering. As I looked him over I had the strangest feeling concerning him that I had ever had in looking into the face of a stranger. I left the platform and walked back to him. His keen eyes almost struck through me. I laid my hand on him and said, "Young man, the devil is using you to do dirt," and turned and walked away. That was one of the most peculiar experiences I ever had. But God used that statement some way to send an arrow of conviction to his precious heart. For seventeen days B. F. McLendon literally rolled and groaned and wallowed, but God's hook stayed in him, and he couldn't shake it off. I was sure God had marked that boy for a great preacher, and God knows whom He wants. Sometimes He has to wait a number of years for His man but sooner or later God will land him. If anyone who reads this has never heard him, if he comes within five hundred miles of your town, you go to hear him, for you never will regret it.

Brother Huff and I, after working all the southern states in January of 1908 made our way back North. While Brother Huff went to Sioux City for a two weeks' visit with his wife and children, I went to Chicago and had one of the greatest meetings I ever had in my life, where I did all the preaching for Rev. C. E.

Cornell, who was at that time pastor of the First Church of the Nazarene. When we made the first coast-to-coast campaign with Dr. Fowler, Brother Cornell lived in Cleveland, Ohio, and was publishing a little paper called the Soul Winner. He hired me to write for the Soul Winner. He was the first man who ever paid me for writing for a paper. That was the opening of my writing for papers and journals. I made my start with Brother Cornell but the next year Brother Morrison hired me to write for the Pentecostal Herald, and for ten years I wrote what was known as "Bud Robinson's Corner." When we begin to write and think over our trips, how many great and good men stand out in our lives. There is no way to tell what the life and influence of one good man like C. E. Cornell has meant to the world. From January, 1903, until the present Brother Cornell and I have been like David and Jonathan. For many years he has been my pastor.

I left Chicago the middle of January headed for the Northwest and the night I left Chicago Rev. Will Huff left Sioux City. We met the next morning in St. Paul, Minnesota. We had a good hugging spell, for we had not seen each other for two or three weeks. There we secured our sleepers and through tickets from St. Paul, Minnesota, to Everett, Washington. There we had some fine meetings in the old holiness tabernacle. A few years before that Rev. I. G. Martin and Milton Williams had held some great conventions through the Northwest and had organized the Holiness Association and built a very large holiness tabernacle. At that time Brother Sherwood, a fine school teacher, was president and Sister Lewis, the wife of a good doctor, was secretary, and we were called to Everett by the president and secretary of the association.

At the close of this great convention we found that we had more meetings to hold than we had time to stay in the Northwest, so we divided, and Brother Huff went to Greenlake, a suburb of Seattle, and held a meeting for Brother McKinley, one of the finest Free Methodist preachers in the nation. While he was there I went back to the beautiful little town called Snohomish, nestling on the banks of the Snohomish river, near the foothills of those gigantic Cascade mountains, whose tops are so high that it seems that they would tickle the bottoms of the angels' feet if they were to sit on the doorsteps and swing their feet off. I held my meeting for Brother Sayres, a fine Methodist Episcopal preacher, and stayed in the home of Brother and Sister Seeley. They also had a fine preacher boy at that time stationed at Bellingham, on the northern border of Washington, a few miles from the Canadian line, and he came down and stayed with us a few days. He and I became warm friends. I remember while I was in Snohomish, that the little fish called the smelt, came up the streams and rivers. The reader may think I am out of my mind or this is an exaggeration, but the farmers backed their wagons into the rivers and took their forks and loaded the wagons with these fish and hauled them out onto the ground for fertilizer, notwithstanding they are the best fish I ever put down my neck, and anybody who ever ate those smelt in Oregon and Washington while they are fresh, will agree that they are the limit for goodness. Brother and Sister Seeley had gone to Washington in early days from western New York, where their relatives still live. They had been back on a visit and brought back West a big cake of maple sugar. They gave me a block of it that weighed two pounds. I wrapped that up and carried it in my suitcase until I reached home in Peniel, Texas, the first day of April.

At the close of my meeting in Snohomish I went to Seattle, where Dr. Reese, pastor of the First Methodist church, was at that time building the great First Methodist church and they had erected a large tabernacle to worship in until their church was completed. The holiness association of Seattle secured this big tabernacle for us to hold a great convention in and Dr. Reese, the pastor, joined in with us and we had there a very remarkable convention. One of the leading men then in the First Methodist church was Tom Lippe, who had become a millionaire by operating gold mines in the Klondike. He and his wife went out among the first ones when the gold rush opened up in the Klondike and Mrs. Tom Lippe was the first woman to go into the gold mines. At the close of our convention Brother Lippe requested that we be paid off in gold and we had more gold than we probably ever had before or since at one time. At that time Brother R. L. Wall was president of the Holiness Association in Seattle and at this writing he is president of the Southern California Holiness Association. He has been a personal friend of mine for twenty-seven years. He is a traveling shoe

man, one of the most cultured Christian gentlemen that
you will meet in a lifetime.

At the close of our great convention in Seattle,
Brother Huff, Brother Wall, Brother McKinley and
this writer planned a trip by boat down through Puget
Sound and up to Victoria in British Columbia. It is
the most beautiful city in the Northwest and is the capital of British Columbia. Our trip was lovely. We
got there in time to take in the state house and we
spent the night in the King Edward's hotel. The next
morning we went back to Seattle and went out in the
afternoon to the home of Brother Tom Lippe to a big
holiness meeting that was held by Sister Lippe. Brother Huff made a talk and there were nine women at the
altar for sanctification.

From Seattle we went down to Portland, Oregon,
and gave one afternoon and night to Brother A. O.
Henricks, who had just taken charge of the Church of
the Nazarene that had been organized only a few weeks
before. We had two great services and from there we
went to Ashland, Oregon, for a ten days' meeting. We
had a fine revival there and met a number of good
people who have been warm friends of mine from that
day until this. One of them was good Brother Rice,
who worked for a number of years in our Publishing
House. He is now in Southern California but with the
same smile on his face.

From Ashland we made our next stop in Oakland,
California. Here Brother P. G. Linaweaver was pastor. Brother Huff and I had worked with him in Illinois

a year before. He had come from another church to the Church of the Nazarene. He took us across the bay to the headquarters of the great Southern Pacific railroad system to their general passenger agent and got us clergy rates from San Francisco to Los Angeles with a ten days' stop over and from there to Greenville, Texas. We had two beautiful days with Brother Linaweaver.

We came from there to Los Angeles and held a meeting for Dr. P. F. Bresee, closing on the last Sunday of March. While I was there I learned that Dr. Bresee wanted to go East and I asked him to come through Texas and come to Peniel and organize a Nazarene church. He said he would do that. He asked me how many I thought would come in. I told him I thought there would be a number, but I knew for sure there would be one for he could take me in. He said that would be worth the trip.

I reached home on the first day of April. I had notified my wife that I was going to present her an April Fool on the first day of the month and sure enough my train pulled in just before midnight on April first. She met me at the train with my two beautiful girls, little Sally and baby Ruby. I notified the people that Dr. Bresee was coming and two days later he arrived and preached for us until the first Sunday of April. On Sunday night, April the sixth, he organized the first Church of the Nazarene in the state of Texas. At that time Dr. E. P. Ellyson, who is now the editor of the Sunday school literature of the Church of the

Nazarene, assisted by his good wife, was the college president. Today he is one of the best Sunday school editors in the United States of any denomination. I doubt whether there is any better Sunday school literature published in the world than is sent out by our headquarters at Kansas City, Missouri. Dr. Bresee organized with 103 members, and thank the Lord the Nazarene work was started in Texas.

CHAPTER VIII

In 1907 the Association of Pentecostal Churches of the East and the Church of the Nazarene of the West had met in Chicago and had united, and become one church under the name of Pentecostal Church of the Nazarene. Brother C. B. Jernigan, who has been and who is today one of the most untiring workers in the Southwest, went from the South to Chicago and met with them in the union of those two bodies. At that time he was at the head of the Holiness Church of Christ. Through the influence of Brother Jernigan plans were made for their next General Assembly to meet in September of 1908, in Pilot Point, Texas. There the various bodies of holiness people united, and all took the name of the Pentecostal Church of the Nazarene, which name it held until 1919 when the word Pentecostal was dropped and they brought it back to the first name that Dr. Bresee had given it when he organized it in Los Angeles, October 20, 1895. The name then was given as The Church of the Nazarene. While we are commonly called the Nazarene Church that is not our name. Let it be remembered for all time that the name of this church is The Church of the Nazarene. That is the most beautiful name in the whole world, for in Matt. 2:23 we read this remarkable statement: "And he came and dwelt in a city called Nazareth: that it might be fulfilled which was spoken by the prophets, He shall be called a Nazarene." We have the most beautiful name in the world for our church. Not only was Jesus a Nazarene but we also have the apostle Paul. All denominations claim St. Paul but the Nazarenes are the people that have really got him. In proof of that read Acts 24:5: "For we have found this man a pestilent fellow, and a mover of sedition among all the Jews throughout the world, and a ringleader of the sect of the Nazarenes." Some good people have told us that we did harm because we belonged to a sect and have tried to prove their doctrine by St. Paul. But we are the crowd that have him.

During this great assembly in Pilot Point Dr. E. P. Ellyson was elected one of the General Superintendents. Before that Dr. P. F. Bresee and Dr. H. F. Reynolds were the two General Superintendents, but in the fall of 1908 Dr. E. P. Ellyson was elected General Superintendent also. During that assembly the plans were made to invade the beautiful old Southland. The next General Assembly was set for three years ahead to meet in the fall of 1911 in Nashville, Tennessee, with our good Brother J. O. McClurkan, the founder of the Pentecostal Mission; the founder also of our school in Nashville, Trevecca College. He was then editor of the paper called Living Water. Since that time our good Brother McClurkan has gone to live with Jesus. It is wonderful how God has raised up great and good men but it seems strange that then He should translate them when apparently they were right in the most useful period of their lives. But He has always planned some other man should take up the work and carry it on. It was so at Nashville, it has been so everywhere else.

When the time came for the General Assembly to meet, behold the delegates were there from California, and Washington and Oregon and from the West and Northwest, and from far-off Maine, and all the Eastern and Northern states were represented. This was one of our greatest General Assemblies. It was the first one after the various branches of the holiness movement had united. Two bodies united in 1907 in Chicago; two other bodies united in 1908, and by 1911 the great work of the Pentecostal Church of the Nazarene, not only was reaching out to the entire United States but it was beginning to reach out to the foreign fields. Today the Church of the Nazarene has girdled the globe. From that General Assembly we went out to all quarters of the nation, and many missionaries were there from almost every mission field.

God has brought the various bodies of the holiness movement together until, while they are not all in one body as a church, they are one in doctrine and experience, and as to their church government there is but little difference. We are one great body of believers. If there were a union of Nazarenes, Pilgrim Holiness, Wesleyan Methodist and Free Methodists there would be nearly 150,000 people, every one of them believing in a whole Bible for a whole world and a salvation from all sin for all men through the atoning blood of Jesus Christ. We may not live to see this great union but it is very likely that before many years at least the most of these good people will be in one great body, in order that they may defend the Bible and the faith of our fathers. In fact, as this old man sees it, we need only two Protestant churches in America. We firmly believe that all people who believe every word of the Bible could be in one great denomination, and we see no reason why all of that crowd who have found so many mistakes in the Bible should not be in one great church, for there is no difference in their lives and conduct, and as far as we can see there is no difference in their faith. This would make up two Protestant churches of the United States.

Going back a few years, there has been in my mind a peculiar feeling that I ought to write up a dream that I had once, or probably a vision. I have hesitated because I have never been visionary, but after all a man doesn't have to be a visionary man to have visions. As a rule when a man has a vision he gets busy and works it out; while on the other hand a visionary man apparently never gets anything done.

A number of years ago while I was holding a meeting, in a dream I was carried back to Georgetown, Texas, and was in the little home, a beautiful cottage that belonged to my wife when she and I were married. It seemed to me that I arose very early one morning (and walked out from that cottage a few miles to the mountains.) Everything was lovely, the flowers were in bloom, the birds were singing, the dewdrops were hanging from every leaf and every twig of grass. I had never seen a more beautiful morning in my life. (As I strolled through the woods I could see the bees gathering honey and the birds were singing and making such

melody that it seemed) all the earth was full of music.
I walked to the top of a beautiful mountain where I
had never been before. Off to the west there lay before
me a great valley; it looked to be a mile deep and several miles wide. Across the valley there was another
mountain running parallel with the one I stood on and
I could see up and down that valley for miles. The sun
was coming up over the mountains and as I looked up
that valley it seemed to me that I could see a wall of
black, muddy water rolling down the valley (until it
seemed it would fill the valley to the top of each mountain. It came slowly down the valley and when it came
within about one mile to my right I could hear the roar
of the water. (I couldn't imagine where such a flood of
muddy water had come from but when it came nearer,
instead of being the roar of the water it was shrieks
and wails and groans and to my sad surprise the Lord
showed me that that valley was full of precious, immortal souls (who were rolling just like black, muddy
water.) I looked and it seemed like a few hundred
yards to my left in the twinkling of an eye those mountains and that valley were cut in two and the mountain
and valley cut off seemed to flee miles and miles into
the distance. I could see them disappearing and then
there was a gulf left that looked to be thousands of
miles in every direction,) a chasm without a bottom.
Then I saw that the river of immortal souls was going
to go over that awful precipice into that chasm. I began to scream to them at the top of my voice to stop,
that just a little way down was the awful chasm, but

they paid no attention to me. I saw something must be done. I ran right into that black, muddy water and grabbed up my arms full of those black, muddy human souls; it seemed that they were almost as large as men but I could carry my arms full of them. I dragged them out and laid them down right on the top of the mountain where I was standing. And when I laid them down they rose up, the most beautiful creatures I had ever seen, robed in white. I didn't stop, but ran back and gathered my arms full again and brought them out and laid them down and they rose up like the others and looked like angels. On I went without stopping until it was high noon and the sun coming on my head was very warm. I was getting tired and was wet with perspiration but on and on that valley was full of black, muddy souls, and on I went and stopped for nothing. I became hungry and thirsty but I never stopped. Just as fast as I could run in and get my arms full and lay them on the mountain, they would rise up like angels and I would go back for another load. Finally it seemed to me I was completely exhausted and didn't see how I could make another trip into that black, muddy river. But as I stood there and gazed at that rolling body of what first seemed to be muddy water their shrieks and wails and groans so pierced my heart that I couldn't stand it and ran back into that muddy river and got my arms full; I dragged them out and laid them down on the bank, and they rose up and stood beside me, the most beautiful creatures I had ever seen. I thought I must make one more trip. I threw myself in and mustered up all the strength I had. I got my arms full and could not lift them up but simply dragged them out and laid them down. I could see their feet at the edge of the water and I could not make another trip. I was wet with perspiration and the muddy water was scattered all over me, I had no strength left and just as I could see the rim of the sun sinking over the mountain I dragged out my last load of precious immortal souls. I lay down on the mountainside to rest a minute and there gathered around me tens of thousands of the most beautiful creatures that my eyes had ever beheld. They were the souls I had dragged out of that muddy river. They sang the most beautiful song I had ever heard and while they were singing and rejoicing it seemed to me like the Lord drew very near to me and said to me, "Your day's work is done." Just as He told me that my work was done I awoke out of my sleep, but beloved, for days and weeks afterward every time I went to sleep I could see those beautiful mountains and that black, muddy river and those precious, immortal souls coming down the valley and into that chasm by the teeming millions, and I could see that scripture: "Strait is the gate, and narrow is the way, which leadeth unto life, and few there be that find it, but broad is the way, that leadeth to destruction, and many there be which go in thereat." Thank the Lord for the many I had pulled out, but many went over the precipice and nobody was pulling them out.

I don't knew whether it was a dream or a vision,

but it has lingered with me for thirty or forty years. Many times since that vision, especially in the last few years in working the districts and touring the states, I have felt like I would have to quit and yet I could look back and see the black, muddy river and say, "Dear Lord, I must run in and drag out one more arm load." But thank the Lord, by His grace and loving mercy I have been able to pull a few out of the river of death.

CHAPTER IX

So far in writing up my story I have said nothing about the books I have written. It might be a good idea here to just give a little sketch of them.

The first book that I wrote was "Sunshine and Smiles." I wrote this book in 1902 and the first edition was gotten out by the Texas Holiness Advocate Publishing Company of Peniel, Texas. We sold out the first edition of 5,000 copies and as you will remember I told you of going to Boston to join Dr. Fowler in the fall of 1902. By the time we had traveled as far west as Chicago, the Christian Witness Company secured the copyright and we enlarged the book some and they got their copyright in 1903. Many editions of this little book have been sold, and it has been a blessing to humanity wherever it has gone. A good portion of my experience has been translated into two or three languages. A portion of it was translated into Chinese and Japanese by some missionaries. Some friends have translated a good part into the Spanish language and given it out in tracts, so the reader will see it has been a blessing.

In 1904 I wrote a little book called "The King's Gold Mine," the conversion and sanctification of the disciples before the day of Pentecost. This little book has had a large sale. That same year I wrote a little booklet, "Walking with God or the Devil, Which?"

This has also had a large sale. In 1905 and also 1906 I wrote a beautiful book that was called, "The Pitcher of Cream." This book was published by Dr. H. C. Morrison along with the other two pamphlets that I had written. "The Pitcher of Cream" is a beautiful, cloth-bound book of 160 pages. When a man goes to writing books and gets it into his blood he must work it out some way, so by 1908 I began to study that remarkable character recorded in John 11th and 12th chapters, the story of Lazarus. By 1909 I had this book ready for the press. Dr. Morrison also brought out this book. It is made up of sixteen chapters: The Sick Man, The Dead Man, The Bound Man, The Entombed Man, The Putrefied Man, Christ Went to Town, Christ the Resurrection and the Life, Christ Inquires for the Dead Man, Christ Sought the Dead Man, He Found Him and Wept Over Him, The First Command to the Church—Take Ye Away the Stone, Lazarus Called out of the Tomb, Lazarus Set Free, Lazarus Feasting with the Lord, Lazarus Persecuted, and Lazarus the Great Soul Winner. I believe this little book has been a blessing to tens of thousands.

By 1912 I was writing another book. I took my time and went through the Bible and found all the beautiful things that transpired on the mountains of sacred history. By 1913 I had my book ready for the press, and the book was named, "Mountain Peaks of the Bible." Dr. Morrison also published this book. This is a very beautiful book which has had a large sale and blessed humanity wherever it has gone. By the time I had "Mountain Peaks of the Bible" on the press I was giving every spare minute of my time to writing a book of sermons. I completed this book early in the fall of 1913. I wrote seventeen sermons. The title of the book is "Honey in the Rock" and was published by God's Revivalist Publishing Company of Cincinnati, Ohio. The headings of these sermons are as follows: Why I Believe in Scriptural Holiness, The Abundant Supply, The Two Works of Grace, The Three Ways, Exploits, A Fixed Heart, Christian Perfection, The Blood of Christ or Our Hope of Heaven, The Holy Anointing Oil, The Dangers of the Soul, The Threefoldness of Salvation, The Blameless Life, Repentance and Danger of Neglecting It, The Necessity of Conversion and Sanctification, The Four Confessions, The Three Last Testimonies and The Eye of God.

The next book that I wrote was "My Hospital Experience." As the reader and my friends know, on the first day of June, 1919, in San Francisco I was struck by an automobile, knocked about thirty feet, was taken up with nine broken bones and dislocated joints. I lay on my back for nearly six months growing my bones back. The devil said I would die and many of my good friends thought I would but I said I would get well and preach holiness all over the United States and I believed around the world. My expenses ran to about $600 per month and I was out of the field six months. I made the best wages I almost ever made in my life while I was lying in the hospital growing my bones back. The money came in to pay all the bills. It came from every quarter of the United States and some from across the ocean. In fact, I went to the hospital with ten dollars and all those bills were paid and I came out with a big rag tied up with money. I won't say here how much it was but it was a large sum. It had been left by my good friends and sent in through the mail. I will not try here to give my hospital experience as it is already in book form published by the Pentecostal Publishing Company at Louisville at 15c each or seven for a dollar. This little pamphlet has had a big sale.

By 1920 I was hammering the keys of my old typewriter again, bringing out another book. This, I think, was one of the most beautiful books I have written. The title of this book is "Bees in Clover." It has nearly two hundred pages, beautifully bound, large, clear type and it is published on the finest quality book paper. This book is published by the Nazarene Publishing House, at 2923 Troost Avenue, Kansas City, Missouri, and was copyrighted in 1921. To my way of thinking there are more beautiful things in this book than any I have ever written.

But no sooner was "Bees in Clover" off the press than I began to gather up beautiful things from the writings of men and women and other things that the Lord has given me as I preached and travelled and by 1924 I had written another book and I gave it the title of "Nuggets of Gold." This book also was published by the Pentecostal Publishing Company of Louisville, Kentucky, of which Dr. H. C. Morrison is president. So the reader will see that I haven't been lazy and have not lain down on the job, but from the day God con-

verted me until this good hour I have had my face set
as a flint to go to heaven and carry everybody I pos-
sibly can with me. So here I am now writing another
book that will in a few weeks be on the press and then
I hope it will be read by my friends by the tens of
thousands from ocean to ocean.

When I began telling about my books you will remember we had come to our great General Assembly in
1911. This was held in the fall. At the close of this
General Assembly, W. B. Yates and I went to Louisville, Kentucky, to hold a meeting for Rev. Howard
Eckel, who was pastor of the First Church of the Nazarene there, and at the same time District Superintendent of Kentucky and Tennessee, so you will see this old
boy had a great job. Then Brother Yates and I had
meetings together off and on for a number of years.
That winter we went to Florida and held meetings in
Webster and Taylorsville and went down as far as Fort
Ogden on the west coast. The Lord gave us some very
great revivals.

In the spring of 1913 we came back from Florida
and had a great meeting in Thompson, Georgia, with
dear Brother Bob Edlemonton and his brother H. L.
but better known as Henry, who came down from Atlanta and stayed with us. If ever four old boys had a
good time it was these Edlemonton fellows and Yates
and Robinson.

From there we made a run to East Liverpool, Ohio.
We had a beautiful room in the home of Brother
Homer Taylor and Sister Pearl, his good wife. Brother
Ben Harker, who at that time was in charge of what is

known as the People's Mission, one among the best I
had ever seen up to that time, stood by us nobly and
we had great crowds to preach to and some of the
hardest cases I think I have almost ever met were gloriously saved in that meeting. Since those good days
our precious Brother Harker has been translated and
has gone to live with Jesus.

At the close of this convention Brother Yates went
to some point in Kentucky and I went to Meridian,
Mississippi, and held a meeting for the Beeson brothers. I was there over Easter Sunday, and Brother
Joseph H. Smith brought a great message on the "Resurrection" on that day. In our two weeks we had over
two hundred and fifty at the altar. Beloved, those were
great days in the holiness movement. If the holiness
movement could have been received by the people
called Methodists I believe that hundreds of thousands
would have been saved and sanctified that will probably
be lost forever. Of course, in those days when people
were driven out of the church for the doctrine and experience of entire sanctification they naturally had to
go to schoolhouses, brush arbors, old storehouses, court-
houses and under the old gospel tents, but thank God
for the tens of thousands that I have seen go down
crying and come up flying, washed in the beautiful
stream.

Beloved, the end is not yet; God is still on the
throne and the government is still on His shoulder, and
of the increase of His government and peace there shall
be no end.

Before I get too far into 1913 I must not forget to

tell you that in 1912 I sold my home in Peniel, Texas, and moved to Pasadena, California. I located on the school grounds of what is now the Pasadena College. My home is on Bresee Avenue at 1169 but I have given but very little time to my home and to this beautiful climate. Of course, the reader will understand that I have come out home about once a year for rest, and evangelistic work for about three weeks up and down the coast. 1914 found me with a slate for three years ahead. Sometimes I received as many as nine hundred calls in a single year, preaching from four to five hundred times a year and travelling from 25,000 to 35,000 miles annually.

In the fall of 1914 Rev. M. Edward Borders, who was then pastor of our church at Malden, Mass., began to write me to give him a great convention in April, 1915. I had so many calls that I didn't see how I could go but finally Dr. C. J. Fowler wrote me one of the most beautiful letters I ever read and pleaded for me to make one more trip through New England, that he wanted to be with me some more before he went up and I finally arranged the date. I worked through Kentucky and Tennessee during the latter part of the winter and early spring. By March I had reached Columbus, Ohio. There we had a handful of members and Brother Robert Kell was their pastor. I went up and while there we secured the big Presbyterian church that they own today. They were unusually kind and gave us such easy terms that it was easy to buy so we bought the church and moved in, but it had been closed up for three or four years and oh, the dust and cobwebs in that building. It took a number of our Nazarene people almost a week to clean it up and if ever two boys worked it was Bob Kell and Bud Robinson. We cleaned up the big stoves in the basement and got everything ready down there. We went to a big grocery merchant and told him we wanted him to supply us with groceries until that meeting closed. He said to us, "Anything that you men want in my store come over and get it," so we marched over and laid in a good supply of groceries, which our good Nazarene women cooked. We had all day meetings for a month and made no charge for meals but we put up a little box in the dining room with a hole in it with the words, Free Will Offerings. During the month we fed up eighty dollars worth of groceries and only served dinner.

I will never forget one rich old Methodist brother from out of town who was at the altar and got blessed. We marched him down to dinner and after he got all the roast beef and mashed potatoes he could eat he said, "Whom do I pay now?" We said, "Sir, the only way we collect money here is in this box, whatever you wish to pay put it in there." He walked up and put a twenty dollar bill through that hole and said, "This is the greatest day of my life; to go to a meeting and get saved and sanctified and have all I can eat and nobody to present a bill beats anything I ever experienced in my life."

During this meeting of a month we had over five hundred at the altar. We took in twice as many members as we had and the offerings came up and overflowed everything. It is remarkable how people give when God comes to town. We hadn't been there long until the boys at the railroad Y. M. C. A. put in a special plea for us to give them one afternoon of each week so we went there and had a great time and the revival reached the railroad shops, and the railroad boys began to request noon meetings, so we would go over there and give them a great rally. I think we went four or five times while in Columbus. During this campaign there were three Presbyterian Sunday school superintendents beautifuly sanctified. In that meeting big Brother Beckett, who had been saved in the Billy Sunday meeting, who had been train caller in the great Pennsylvania railroad station for thirteen years, knelt at the altar and God sanctified him. Bless his memory; in a few years he had been translated. Some two years ago his good wife followed on.

Beloved, it is remarkable the number of people I have seen converted or sanctified that many years ago have gone to live with Jesus. While I am on that point, in Long Beach, California, in the great building on the docks, while we were touring the state in January, 1920, in a coast-to-coast campaign, I gave the story of my life and there were people from twenty-five states and fifty different cities that had been converted or sanctified in my meetings who stood up and testified to it. So you will see that I have got to walk straight. We used to say when we were preaching and the people would jump up and down and shout, that all we required of them was that they walk straight when they came down, so the Lord requires at my hand what I required at the hands of the people.

At the close of the great campaign in Columbus I ran over and gave two days and nights at Marion, Ohio, and from there I went to Boston. I got off the train at the old South Station, and was met by Brother William McDonald and his good wife and a young lady that was keeping house for them and, if I am not mistaken, Brother Border's older daughter, Miss Irene Borders. It was a wonderful trip through Boston in those days in an automobile. I was entertained in the home of Brother McDonald and there the Lord gave us a most glorious revival. I will nveer forget the scenes around the altar. The people became so interested that they would come to church and fill the church almost an hour before preaching would begin and when I would come over the only way I could get in would be to go around and come into the church through the big door that opened into the parsonage. I don't think I ever worked with a man in all my experience that had a greater influence in the city than Brother Borders had. He had a fine backing in his church. One of the most cultured gentlemen of New England, Brother Peavy, was the chairman of his church board and Borders and Peavy were like Jonathan and David. To me Brother Borders was one of the most interesting preachers I had ever met. He told me some days nothing could be done while maybe within twenty-four hours the same thing that could not have been done the day before could be done. He said, "Brother Bud, you have got to do everything at the psychological minute." I had carried with me my trunk packed full of books and people began to call for

them, but Brother Borders would shake his head and
say, "I will tell you when to open it. When the psychological minute comes I will notify you." So one
night when we had the house packed until they were
standing around the walls, Brother Borders came in
with a big grin and his eyes sparkling and said, "Un-
lock your trunk at once; the psychological minute has
arrived." I opened my trunk and within a few minutes
he sold every book and had orders for fifty more and
we wired Chicago to send them next mail. He had just
remodeled his big church and had it newly decorated
until it was a beauty and he needed $1500 to pay up
that bill. One Sunday morning he walked up and said,
"The psychological moment has arrived," and laid his
watch on the pulpit and in ten minutes the people had
given him $1800.

But going back just a little before that when Brother Borders had taken the church, if my memory serves
me correctly, there was a mortgage for $7,000 and that
old boy had raised every dollar of that and paid it and
burnt it and had had his church remodeled for the Robinson campaign.

The first two weeks I was with him we had some
great noon meetings at the city hall. There was a
young man that worked with him that was named
Robinson though no kin to Bud. The last week that I
was with Brother Borders the New England District
Assembly met in his church. The people came from
all over New England; he had good homes for everyone
and fine entertainment. I have never seen a District
Assembly entertained in my life better than it was at

that time. Dr. H. F. Reynolds, General Superintendent, presided at this great assembly and Brother Washburn was District Superintendent. It was at this assembly that they elected delegates to the General Assembly to meet in Kansas City in the fall. It was very interesting and I remember good Brother Lanpher, who is pastor of our First church in Portland, Maine, got up and offered a resolution to memorialize the General Assembly to drop the word Pentecostal from their name and go back to the first name that Dr. Bresee gave the church when it was organized, and take the name The Church of the Nazarene. They had some mighty interesting speeches. I think that the motion put before the assembly was lost, but I thought it was beautiful for the brethren of the East who were the founders of the Pentecostal Church to memorialize the assembly to drop the word Pentecostal from the church name. They gave for their reason that the great band of Pentecostal people called the unknown tongues people were known far and wide by that name and that many people had somehow confounded the Nazarenes with the other folks. But the name was not dropped until the General Assembly in Kansas City in 1919. There the word was dropped and the church has been known as "The Church of the Nazarene" until the present time. We had at that great assembly our beloved Brother George Franklin who was outgoing missionary to India. He made a very great missionary speech and called mourners and filled the altar.

At the close of this assembly I rested up for a couple of days and then went to Lowell, Mass., where our beloved Brother Riggs and Brother Beers were the pastors of the great church there. I was with the brethren thirteen days and we had a real good convention. My home at that time was with a fine family by the name of Cove. Miss Mary Cove has been an active missionary worker in this country. From there I went down to Portsmouth, Virginia, and held a meeting in the First Friends church. At that time Brother Claude Rome was pastor. My recollection is that he stayed at that church for nine years, and before that Brother C. H. Babcock, of national fame as preacher, orator and writer, was pastor for seven successive years. The Lord gave me a fine meeting with Brother Rome. I suppose if I were to try to describe every meeting that I held, it would make this book entirely too large.

From the east coast of Virginia I made my way back into Ohio. During the summer I was on about seven great camp grounds; visiting Roscoe, Ohio; Jamestown, North Dakota; Red Rock, Minnesota; Indian Springs, Georgia; Wichita, Kansas; and on from place to place until late in the fall. I held campmeetings right up until the General Assembly in Kansas City, then after that went on with my work as before.

CHAPTER X

I think from then during 1916, 1917, 1918, and up till 1919, when I was smashed up, were as hard years as I have gone through in my life. During 1916 I preached, my book shows, nearly five hundred times and traveled 25,000 miles and prayed with between four and five thousand people at the altar. In the summer of 1916 Rev. L. Milton Williams and I were the called workers for the campmeeting at Alexandria, Indiana. There we planned to buy a big gospel tent and open up in the spring of 1917. So we had a very busy summer and in the fall we raised money to buy the big tent.

From the Alexandria camp I went to the camp-meeting at Vincent Springs, Tennessee, out a few miles from Dyersburg. My wife and Ruby joined me in that campmeeting and we had ten days there together. We ran from there to Nashville. I preached a time or two in the old Pentecostal Mission while my wife and Ruby girl had a good visit with our good friend, Sister Kittie Campbell Moore.

They made their way back from Nashville by Kansas City to California, while I turned east again to Portsmouth, Virginia. There I was joined by Brother and Sister Rinebarger and held a four weeks' campaign for Brother Rome in the First Friends church. We had a wonderful revival and took fifty people into the Friends church.

We moved from there over to Norfolk, and went to the First Church of the Nazarene. At that time Brother J. W. Henry was pastor. We had a two weeks' meeting with Brother Henry and from there went to Newport News, First Friends church with Brother Handy. This also was a great convention. We put in altogether eight weeks in those east coast cities. I think there were more fine fish and oysters and good vegetables around Portsmouth, Norfolk and Newport News than any place I had ever visited. We made a run from Newport News to Washington, D. C., and spent two days with Brother L. B. Williams, who was pastor of the Church of the Nazarene in Baltimore, but we spent two days sightseeing in Washington and opened the battle in the city of Baltimore. The Lord gave us a splendid revival.

From there we ran to Philadelphia and gave Brother Maybury, who is now District Superintendent of Washington-Philadelphia District, a week's convention. No finer man on earth than Maybury. While we were there we visited the home of the Ladies' Home Journal and were shown through the great office that was occupied by Mr. Bok, the world famous editor of the Ladies' Home Journal. He had thirty-six other editors and three thousand six hundred at work in that great building, Independence Square. There we saw the old Liberty Bell and where they signed the Declaration of Independence.

We went from there to Huntington, West Virginia,

with Brother John F. Woods, the pastor at that time of the International Holiness church. Since then there has been a union of the International Holiness church with the Pentecostal Pilgrim church; the International boys leaving off the word International and the Pilgrims leaving off the word Pentecostal, making it the Pilgrim Holiness Church. We found Brother Woods a very beautiful brother and God gave us a wonderful revival. He had one of the largest churches in the denomination, and a fine people.

At the close here the Rinebargers went back to their home in New Albany, Indiana, and I went to Cincinnati for Thanksgiving day, as I was one of the workers for a number of days on those occasions at the Bible School. Nearly eight thousand were fed in a single day. From Cincinnati I crossed the continent again, landing in Pasadena the first of December.

For January I turned north. Rev. A. M. Bowes, our good Nazarene pastor in Yakima, Washington, had secured a large theatre and had called Rev. C. H. Babcock and Brother Arthur Ingler for a four Sundays' campaign. Dr. Babcock and the writer did the preaching and Brother Ingler led the choir and brought many of those beautiful solos such as only Arthur Ingler can. During this campaign there were more than five hundred people at the altar. At the close of our great campaign Dr. Babcock went east and I stayed over for two or three days with Brother Bowes and we put on a campaign to raise money to build the new church and before that year was up Brother Bowes had a nice church.

From Yakima I made a run to Calgary, Alberta, Canada. There I joined Brother L. Milton Williams. The Lord gave us a great campaign; scores of precious souls were saved and sanctified. Rev. E. E. Martin, of New England, who is now our good pastor at Worcester, Mass., was then pastor in Calgary. Brother Martin is a noble character. At the close of our meeting in Calgary, we ran down to Portland, Oregon, and preached for two or three days with the Nazarenes and Free Methodists and had a splendid visit with our old friends in Portland.

From there Brother L. Milton Williams made a trip to Oskaloosa, Iowa, to his home for a week or two of rest and I came down the coast and joined my family for a couple of weeks' rest. By April the first we had gotten our band of workers together and our great tent and living tents were all completed and as they were built in Wichita, Kansas, we opened our tent campaign the first Sunday of April in Arkansas City, Kansas. Then for the next eighteen months we were the Williams and Robinson Tent Party. I suppose no band of workers ever had a finer party than the Williams and Robinson Party.

In our first meeting Brother Kenneth Wells had come down from Oskaloosa with Brother Williams and led the singing for one month but at the close of the campaign on the last Sunday of April he went back to Oskaloosa to finish up his study for the month of May and get his diploma from the voice department. Our next campaign was in Oklahoma City for the month of May. We shipped our stuff and had it up by the first

Sunday of May. It took about a week to get ready. At that time Dr. Widmeyer was president of the Oklahoma College and Professor London was his assistant. During this Oklahoma campaign Professor London led the singing and his wife presided at the piano and God gave us a wonderful meeting. In this campaign Miss Virginia Shaffer was converted and sanctified and joined the Williams and Robinson party as our great solo singer. In this meeting Miss Lou Jane Hatch, one of the greatest workers in the city, also joined the party. While we were in Arkansas City in April, I ran down to Blackwell to an all-day meeting and the song service was in charge of Professor John E. Moore, and I said, "There is the man to lead the choir for the Williams and Robinson Evangelistic Party. We arranged for this fine man to go with us to Wichita, Kansas, for the month of June.

We pulled down and shipped there and by the first Sunday of June we had gathered together a band of workers that stayed for a year. Brother and Sister Hipple had joined us at the beginning. He was the property manager and Sister Hipple had charge of the dining room. Then we had secured Miss Eunice Oakes of Indianapolis to join us the first of June as our pianist and Professor Kenneth Wells was to come back and play the trombone. Miss Lou Jane Hatch and Brother Howard Williams were employed and were both to play the violins. Then with Miss Oakes at the piano, Professor Moore leading the choir, Professor Wells with trombone, Miss Hatch and Mr. Williams with violins and Milton Mosch, a German boy, with his cornet and Miss Virginia Shaffer to sing solos and Williams and Robinson to preach we had a great party of workers. I have never seen them surpassed. In fact, I doubt if I have ever seen them equaled as an evangelistic party. John Moore could beat any man to lead a choir I had ever seen; Professor Wells was the best on the trombone that I had ever seen; Miss Oakes could make a piano talk; Milton Mosch was good on a cornet and Miss Hatch and Mr. Williams were good on the violin; Miss Shaffer was in a class by herself when it came to singing. Brother Williams preached every night and Bud Robinson every day.

We went from Wichita, Kansas, to the beautiful city of Topeka, Kansas. There the Lord gave us a great campaign. From there we went to Lincoln, Nebraska, where we had a great campaign and when we finished up in Lincoln Professor Wells and Miss Eunice Oakes wanted to enter school in Oskaloosa.

During our stay in Wichita the Williams and Robinson party had a great ten-passenger car built by the Jones Company, but they could not deliver this car until the last of September. We received it in time to plan a great campaign in San Antonio, Texas, where we could reach the soldier boys, so we shipped our tents to San Antonio. One man in our party that I overlooked was our publicity man, Rev. Stephen Williams. He was one of the best advertisers that I had ever seen. He arranged these big campaigns and got out all the advertising matter. He went on to San Antonio with all of our tents while the rest of us got into our big car and went to Oskaloosa and stayed for a week and rested up and then drove through to San Antonio, Texas, a trip of about 1400 miles. We stopped a few days in Oklahoma City and took in our District Assembly. From there we drove on to San Antonio. When we got there Brother Williams had everything in good shape and we opened up a great campaign. We stayed in San Antonio until the last of February, 1918. Rev. Henry Wallin was pastor, and he stood by the big tent campaign most nobly.

From there we shipped to Austin, Texas, where Rev. E. W. Wells was our good pastor and we had a great campaign. We ran there until April. Then we pulled our big tent down and shipped it to Des Moines, Iowa, and then our good party broke up on the last Sunday of April until the first Sunday in July when we opened in Des Moines. We drove through to Oklahoma City with our band of workers stopping two or three days with Brother Upchurch at Arlington, Texas, at the Berachah Home and also at Peniel, Texas, and gave them one Sunday. We also went by Sherman and gave them two days and nights and by that time the great rains had overtaken us and we made it from Sherman, Texas, to Oklahoma City by train, most of us, while Brother Williams and some of the boys came through by car. There the regular party broke up for a month. Brother Williams and I went on to Wichita and had the big car overhauled and had some improvements made on it. I went home for a little rest while he went to Oskaloosa. But when he got to Oskaloosa he found the big tent would have to be treated. I came back from California and John E. Moore came from his home in Oklahoma and joined me at Bloomington, Iowa, and there he and I ran a good campaign in June, and it was nearly July before we got under the big tent in Des Moines.

When we finished up there the last of July we shipped to Hammond, Indiana, with Brother Balsmeier, the pastor of the Nazarene church for the month of August. Then we shipped from there to Bluffton, Indiana, for September. There Brother Clyde Greene was pastor. We closed up there the last Sunday of September and stored the big tent. That was the last campaign we ever had under the big brown tent. At the close of this meeting the workers disbanded and all went to their homes.

I went from Bluffton to Nampa, Idaho, and assisted in a big tent meeting and at the close of that campaign, about the time that I boarded the train for Pasadena on the way to California I took the flu. Perhaps you will remember the flu came in the fall of 1918. It was just about universal and it was no respecter of persons. Rich and poor, black and white, red, brown and yellow, all died alike.

CHAPTER XI

We lost the fall of 1918 for nearly ninety days. Dr. A. O. Henricks had secured me to hold a meeting in First church, Los Angeles, during the month of January. I recommended John Moore for song leader and they secured him. Brother and Sister Moore came out from Oklahoma and joined me in Pasadena and stayed a day or two and we opened up the first of January. There were still some cases of flu and we put in a day of prayer and fasting and the flu gave way, and the people apparently got well. Then we had a great revival in old First church, the mother church.

I held meetings in and around Southern California up till the last of May. We had a great revival in Brother Cornell's church, the First church of Pasadena, in February. Miss Shaffer came out to California for this meeting.

We had a great closing up in Pasadena and from there Rev. E. G. Roberts, then pastor of our church in Pomona, called me to do the preaching and Miss Shaffer for song service and God gave us a most wonderful revival. From there Rev. I. M. Ellis, who was then pastor in Holtville, in Imperial Valley, called us to hold him a meeting. Brother W. E. Ellis was living there at the time and B. F. Neely was in the valley then and all hands of us had a great revival there. From there we came back up and gave one day to Brother Cornell in First church in Pasadena and the people came until the police put them out. Then we went to Los Angeles for an all-day meeting and from there we went down and had a good revival in Venice, California, where Jim Black was pastor.

At the close of this meeting Miss Virginia went back East and I gave one day to the preachers' meeting in Los Angeles First Methodist church of which Dr. Locke was pastor. We had one of the greatest days that I have ever seen. I had been requested by the preachers to preach on the conversion of the disciples before the day of Pentecost. We had one hundred and fifty preachers in that meeting and many of the professors from the great Southern California University. Dr. Locke came and led me to the pulpit and said, "Brother Robinson, there is not one string on you; be just as free as in your own meetings." Dr. Locke is a beautiful gentleman. At the next general conference he was elected bishop. At the close of that service I was called to twenty-five churches in and around Los Angeles but I couldn't go to any of them. One preacher said at the close, "It will take me a month to get my theology straight for I have been preaching that the disciples were not converted until the day of Pentecost and now I will have to change my theology."

From Los Angeles I made my way up the valley to San Francisco and while there preaching with C. E. Cornell and Brother Shelby Corlett leading the singing in the First Church of the Nazarene, of which Rev. Donnell J. Smith was pastor, it was there on Sunday night, June 1, 1919, that I was broken up by the big automobile.

There is no use to say anything here about that smash-up, as it is in a pamphlet and I have already referred to it in another place in this book. But I was on my back the most of the time until late in the fall. When I got out of the hospital I stayed at home a little while but had to go back to my doctor every day for treatment. Finally he told me that if I would get out and go to preaching I would improve faster than any other way, so the first of November I left Pasadena, California, on a through train for Boston. However, I stopped off in Chicago, reaching there on Saturday and was met by Brother Schurman and taken to the home of my old friend, F. M. Messenger. During the afternoon he took me to see a good doctor and my arm that was still giving me a great deal of trouble was dressed by the doctor, while I talked to him about his soul. Brother Messenger told me a year later that the doctor always referred to what I said to him.

I spent one Sunday in the First Church of the Nazarene. That was one great day. In the morning Sister Stella Crooks brought a great message. In the afternoon I sat in a chair and tried to give them my hospital experience. I will never forget how the good people wept and cried. At night Brother Schurman preached on the subject of the sin against the Holy Ghost and as I had heard no preaching then for several months, it seemed to be one of the most powerful and terrific messages I had ever heard.

There is no man living that can describe the scene

that took place at the altar. The people came from every part of that great church; I have never heard such wailing in my life. One case I can't forget; a big bald-headed man came running down the aisle as fast as he could run with both hands in the air, and if he had been sliding into the pit of eternal despair his wails could not have been more fearful and awful than they were. When he got within a few feet of the altar he seemed to give a leap into the air and fell over the chancel rail and Brother F. M. Messenger ran to him and got his arms around him. I have never heard a man pray louder, or weep more than that bald-headed man did for almost an hour. I have never seen a more desperate battle in any church or camp ground in my ministry. It seemed that the devil had him in his grip and refused to turn him loose. After an hour's awful battle he got up straight on his knees and got his arms around Brother Messenger and wept with his head on his shoulder. He said, "God has won out in this awful battle and I am one time more free from the clutches of the devil." He said, "For a long time I have been a backslider and under such awful condemnation that when I would go down the street and look at this church my poor heart would almost break. Now, thank God, He has restored the sweet peace to my heart." Fifteen or twenty people prayed through that night. That was on Sunday night, November 9, 1919. After preaching Brother Messenger took me home with him and we had a great talk that night and early next morning we were up and had prayers and Brother Messenger and Brother Harry and Sister Mabel drove me to his big publishing house where he makes the Scripture text calendars. It was very interesting to see how they are made. He was turning them out by the million I think. After going through this big publishing plant Brother Harry Messenger took me in the big car to the station. I had a through ticket to Boston and a good Pullman and he was good enough to put me in my good berth; told me good-by and I saw him go down the steps of my Pullman. When it comes to good folks there is no way this side of heaven to improve on these Schurman and Messenger families. They surely are sacks of salt for the hungry sheep to lick at, and pans of honey for the bees to gather around.

I had a nice trip across the great northeast part of our great country and pulled into Boston on Tuesday about noon, November 11. I went downstairs and into the ground to get a subway, a lightning express, as they are called, and we went through that dark tunnel fairly flying. It wasn't long until they told me I had reached my destination. I was on my way to Cambridge, Mass., where I was to join Brother Ruth, Will H. Huff, Kenneth Wells and wife for a great convention in the First Evangelical church. When I slowly poked up that long flight of stairs and came out of that hole in the ground, thank the Lord, there was a kind-looking policeman standing at the top of the steps. I told him what number and street I wanted to go to and he called a taxi and put me in with all the loving kindness of a Christian brother.

In a few minutes the taxi driver unloaded me at the home of Brother and Sister Burns; for twenty-five

years he had been a presiding elder in the Evangelical
Church. When it comes to loving kindness he and his
wife are simply the limit. I was so weak and tired; I
still had one lame leg and a very bad arm. But precious
old Mother Burns dressed that arm every day and they
were taking care of me as though I was in a great hospital. May God bless the memory of these holy saints.
If they have not yet gone to the New Jerusalem they
are not very far from the gates.

That night I met Brother Ruth, Brother Huff and
Brother and Sister Wells for the first time that I had
seen them since I had been broken up the first day of
June. There is no way to tell how my heart rejoiced
when I saw those holy brethren. I remember when
Paul was making his trip to Rome after months of suf-
fering and hardship we read that when he saw the
Three Taverns he took courage, and when I saw that
band of holy saints my heart leaped for joy.

Our convention there was one of power and glory.
The holy people came from all parts of that Boston
country. Bands of students came over from the college
at Wollaston, Massachusetts. At the close of this convention we went to Lowell, Massachusetts. We held a
meeting in the First Church of the Nazarene of which
my old friend, Rev. John Gould, and his beautiful wife,
Sister Olive Gould, were in charge. Brother A. L.
Whitcomb was closing a big convention in that church
with Brother Gould. He preached for us on Monday
night and our convention opened Tuesday night. Some
good saint may read this and remember that Lowell is

the home of that old saint, Brother Riggs. I suppose no more beautiful saint has ever lived on earth.

By the time we closed this convention we had more work outlined than we had time to do, and as Brother Ruth had found that he could secure Brother Gouthey and wife he sent Rev. Will H. Huff and Brother Gouthey and wife to Lynn to a great convention there, while Brother Ruth, the Wells and I went to Perkasie, Pennsylvania. We held a convention there in the First Evangelical church. Perkasie is a small town on the Reading and Philadelphia Railroad thirty-five miles north of Philadelphia, but I give you that piece of history to lead up to the facts that I want you to know. Just out a mile or two from this little city in a beautiful little rich valley Rev. C. W. Ruth was born and reared, saved and sanctified and called to preach in that little town. Beloved, the thing that makes the little city of Nazareth in the Holy Land famous is not the age of the city, though it is very old. It is not the size of its population, but the fact that the boy Jesus grew up there. The fact that the blessed Christ was born in a manger in the city of Bethlehem makes it one of the most famous and honored cities in the known world. For the birth of Jesus Christ has changed the history of the world and has changed all of the calendars and has changed the heading on every legal paper, for all notes must have the birthday of Jesus Christ on them or the money could never be collected. As great as was Moses, God's great law giver, as great as was St. Paul, God's greatest theologian on earth, you could not collect money by placing the name of Moses or St. Paul on your paper. Beloved, it is about time for the infidels to keep quiet and somehow be enabled by divine grace to stop up the rat hole in their "noggin" and keep their tongues in their mouths when even if one infidel lends money to another they must put on the note the birthday of Jesus Christ. If it were today they would have to put on their note, February 9, 1927, or their note would not be worth the amount of paper it was written on. Thank God, we believers just take courage and shout on.

A number of Brother Ruth's relatives live in the beautiful city of Perkasie. I had been there once before and at each visit my home was with a beloved brother by the name of Dill. He and his good wife are beautiful saints. The first time I was there I did not have as much joy in preaching as I usually have from the fact that I thought those beautiful old German brethren were displeased with my preaching, for at the close of each service someone would come up and look me right in the face as solemn as the judgment day and say to me, "You said in your sermon that God had turned a hogshead of honey into your soul and that the honey was oozing out between your ribs and that you had just cut a bee tree and that your bees had already swarmed once that day. I want to know what you meant by that." Well, brother, I was up against a proposition, but I would say kindly, "Now, beloved, that is only one of my expressions of joy and hilarity. That is the way I am feeling in my soul." He would nod kindly and walk away. But maybe by the next sermon another old fellow would walk up and say,

"You said today that you were as happy as a bald-headed bumblebee in a hundred acres of red top clover. Now what did you mean?" I would do my best to explain and he would turn and walk away. Maybe by the next time I would finish my discourse another old fellow would walk up and say, "You said today that you could turn a somersault in the big dipper and shave the man in the moon and cut off his hair and hang your hat on the seven stars and put your tie and collar on a flying meteor and march up the milkmaid's path to the New Jerusalem. What did you mean?" Then it was up to me to explain again.

But, thank the Lord, by the close of this meeting eighty people had been saved and sanctified. I left town feeling like I had made a failure but a few years later I was called to North Reading, Pennsylvania, about twenty miles north of Reading, to hold their campmeeting. It is probably seventy-five or one hundred miles from Perkasie, but one day about noon there were nine carloads of those old Dutchmen who came driving up to the camp. They had started in time to get to the morning service but having some trouble were delayed. I had preached in the morning and had announced the other preacher for the afternoon but when dinner was served one of these old fellows walked up and said, "Now you are going to preach this afternoon." I said, "No, I can't do it. I preached in the morning and the other man will preach this afternoon." He said, "Well, the other man will be all right but he is not going to preach. Here all forty of us came to hear you preach and you've got to preach." I said, "I couldn't turn this other man down." He said, "This other man is going to keep quiet," and said, "You are going to preach." Then he looked at me very solemn and said, "We have come to hear you and we want you to make your bees swarm and we want you to tell about the hogshead of honey turned over in your soul and we want you to tell about shaving the man in the moon. We have come all the way to hear you say those beautiful things and we have talked about it ever since you were in Perkasie." Nothing would do them but I must call the other man out and let this beautiful old Dutchman talk to him, and he was glad to get out of it and take the evening service. I had thought these good people were displeased with what I said, but after several years they drove a hundred miles and requested me to preach and give them all those things I had given them in Perkasie. You can't always tell when a good Dutchman is pleased. But one thing is sure, when a Dutchman says yes to God he will come as near standing right there till the day of death as any human being on earth.

But we are back down to Perkasie in our convention. At the close of our convention Brother Ruth had planned for Huff and Gouthey to go to Wilmington, Delaware, while Ruth, Robinson and Wells went to Baltimore. There the International Holiness Church, of which Rev. John Coleman was pastor, and the Free Methodists and the Church of the Nazarene had united for one great convention in Baltimore which was held in the International Holiness church. My home was with Brother Ed Slocum and his good wife and his daughter, Miss Cora. These are among the finest people that have lived on earth, really since Adam died. There is no way to improve on them for manhood, womanhood and Christian integrity. Our beloved Brother John Coleman is now pastor of First Pilgrim Holiness church of Cincinnati, for since that meeting the International Holiness Church and Pentecostal Pilgrim Church have united under the name of the Pilgrim Holiness Church, and Brother Coleman is one of the leading men in that denomination.

At the close of these two conventions, Baltimore and Wilmington, Brother and Sister Gouthey had meetings of their own to conduct and we began again with our first party, Ruth, Huff, Robinson and the Wells, and our next convention was held in Chicago, in Sister Venard's beautiful Bible school known as the Chicago Evangelistic Institute. We had here a most beautiful convention, for anyone would know that in any school like that we would have a great backing. We have no finer lady in the nation than Sister Venard. She is one of God's handmaidens of the earth. When it comes to a great mind and a beautiful character, I suppose Sister Venard is equal to any in the nation. We were well provided for and our convention was one that we will never forget.

Our next convention was held in Lansing, Michigan, in the First Methodist Episcopal church. This was a very great convention. We closed out there on Sunday night before Christmas and Monday morning Will Huff boarded the train for Sioux City, Iowa, to be with his family over the holidays and Brother Ruth and Brother and Sister Wells went to Indianapolis as their homes are in that city. Since I was so far from California I couldn't go home, I stayed in Lansing over the holidays. Our good brother, W. R. Gilley, was pastor of the First Church of the Nazarene in that city and had done as much if not more to get this convention in Lansing than any other one man. He and his good people lined up with us. They stood by us with their presence, their prayers and their pocket books. I gave Brother Gilley four nights and during those four nights we had thirty-two people saved and sanctified. We just exactly averaged eight each night. Such entertainment I have never seen. For the four days we either had a turkey dinner, a goose dinner, a duck dinner, or a great chicken dinner and for these four days Brother Gilley raised me more money than I have often received for a ten days' meeting. God bless the givers.

On Friday I ran down to Indianapolis and Brother Ruth and the Wells gave the last Sunday of December to First Church of the Nazarene. We had one most glorious good time. My home was with Brother Ruth, and there isn't anything but making a trip to the New Jerusalem where you could have a better time than visiting Brother Ruth.

On Monday morning after the last Sunday of December at a very early hour we left Indianapolis for Versailles, Illinois. There we had a fine convention in the First Methodist church. We had many Methodist preachers from that part of the state to visit us. Among the good men who were there, was our old friend, Brother George Oliver, who was for a lifetime connected with old Camp Sychar, Ohio, but today he is in a far better country than this. He has outstripped us and gone to his reward, but he was a great blessing and uplift to the meeting. At the close of our convention, which was the first Sunday of January, 1920, our next convention was to be held in the city of Denver and on the way to Denver we changed cars at the home of the famous Mark Twain. Brother and Sister Wells went up and looked at his old home. As I was still on a lame leg I stayed at the depot and rested. By Tuesday we pulled into Denver and met Brother Huff. Our convention was in a big community church or something of that order of which Dr. Peck was pastor. The Holiness Association of Denver had arranged for this convention. I think the plans were arranged for Mrs. Emma Baller, who is at the present Mrs. Schaeffer, the secretary of the Holiness Association. I had not met her for many years but she had the same old shine on her face and ringing testimony and was doing all in her power to keep second blessing holiness alive. We had there a fine convention and there were many saved.

Our next convention was a long ways from Denver; we had to make a run from Denver to Tacoma, Washington, and while we generally open our conventions every Tuesday night, on this occasion we did not reach Tacoma until Wednesday. There we were in the Evangelical church and had a most glorious time. The people came from Seattle by auto loads and boat loads and from down the railroad as far as Portland. I don't think I had enjoyed a convention up to that time more than I did there. The state of Washington can boast of the finest apples and the finest fish of the nation and for one week we feasted on the red apples, big salmon and little smelts. We all enjoyed our stay very much in Tacoma. They are a most noble people. The Evangelicals are almost all German by nationality and it has been said that when you convert a German three times; get his head, heart and his pocket book converted, that you have got the most noble character living. At this point I want to add that one time Bishop McCabe came nearest to knocking me clear out of the ranch at one blow of anything that ever happened in a religious service. In bringing one of his great messages he made this remark: "I can get two Irishmen converted while I am getting one German converted." I jumped up and shouted as loud as I could and said, "Hurrah for the Irishmen," and the congregation smiled. The old bishop looked very pleasant when he made this remark but he said the one German is worth the two Irishmen when you get him. Well, I was like the boy the calf ran over, and all I could say was, "Lord, help us," and the people laughed until their laughter made the building ring, but I looked down my nose.

But here we are making that Irish detour closing a great convention in Tacoma. From Tacoma we ran down to Portland. There our convention was held in the First Church of the Nazarene of which Brother John T. Little was their faithful pastor. Our convention was one of great interest. We outgrew our churches until we had to change a time or two to get room. Portland, Oregon, is a great apple country and equally as fine fish as they have in Washington, for these two great states border on each other a few miles out from the city of Portland. Vancouver, Washington, is on the north bank of the Columbia river, while Portland is on the south bank. We have no finer band of holiness people than in Portland, Oregon. There were at least two good Free Methodist churches and two or three fine Friends churches to help the Nazarenes boost this convention. Also there are a great many fine holiness people belonging to the Methodist Episcopal churches of that city. The other Nazarene churches in the suburbs of Portland and other towns were in attendance. They came up from Salem and Newberg and Sellwood. We had a great attendance, and unusually fine interest.

We left Portland on January 26, 1920. On January 27, as we were coming over the great mountain range pulling around by the side of Black Butte and Mt. Shasta, we remembered that was my birthday. Brother and Sister Wells and this old writer celebrated my birthday on the top of the mountains in sight of Mt. Shasta. How good the Lord is. We were then headed for San Francisco where we were to hold a convention in one of the large Methodist churches of which at one time Rev. A. C. Baine was pastor. To this day the church is called "A. C. Baine's old church." Beloved, the reason a name will stay with a church like that is because its pastor was a holiness man and it is remarkable how it will get out on a man and people will go for miles and miles to his church and pay no attention to any other. Until this day they talk about Dr. Carradine's old church in St. Louis.   The reason is that Dr. Carradine was one of the greatest holiness preachers in this nation in his day.

It was on June 1, 1919, that I was broken up in San Francisco and I was back the last of January, 1920, and you may remember this, that as this old man tells it, he dreaded the automobile traffic in San Francisco. I was afraid to get out of my room.   Our good Brother Donnell J. Smith was still pastor there and the Nazarene churches in Oakland and Berkeley came over and gave us a boost in this convention.   We had some souls saved but San Francisco is not an open field for the holiness movement.   This fact might help the reader to understand that statement when you remember that out of 800,000 people we have between twelve and fourteen thousand Protestant church members and for every dollar that is given to Jesus Christ they give twelve dollars to Buddha.   We talk about going to the foreign fields to get the heathen converted; it might not be out of order to put on some real conventions among the foreigners of San Francisco.

At the close of our convention we made a run for Los Angeles, California.   Here the Southern California Holiness Association of which R. L. Wall is president and Brother Bert Clark is secretary, had secured the German Methodist church to hold this convention in. This church is a strictly red-hot, second blessing holiness church.   I have known their good pastor for a number of years but there is no way in this world for me to know how to begin to make preparation to see if I could spell his name and I want to be honest enough not to make any attempt, but nevertheless he is a fine brother and if he ever reads this book he will know whom I am talking about. Our convention was very wonderful, our crowds were simply immense. The building was not over half large enough. We had fine entertainment and all of the good help we needed, for Los Angeles is a great church-going city, and with all the good German Methodists, Nazarenes, Evangelicals, Free Methodists, Quakers, Methodist Episcopals and Methodist Episcopals, South, you can get as many holiness people in a convention as any city in America. A good part of the time while there I stayed over at home with my family and went back and forth for the services. However, I had a beautiful room in one of the nice hotels there.

At the close of this great convention we made a run to San Diego. Our convention there was held in the First Church of the Nazarene of which Rev. Joseph Bates was pastor. Our convention was very interesting indeed, for there are many fine holiness people around San Diego. There are some fine Free Methodists, Quakers, Evangelicals and United Brethren that believe in the doctrine and experience of holiness as a second work of grace. At that time our beloved Brother James Elliott was pastor of the First Pentecostal Pilgrim church. He and his good people stood by us nobly. My wife came down a day or two after the opening of this convention and stayed with us. Brother Elliott and his good wife were as kind to wife and me as people could be on earth. While we stayed in our hotel at night they had us out to their home for a number of good meals. He put us in his car and took us over the country between services.

At the close of our convention in San Diego we came back up the coast and had a great convention at Long Beach with Rev. J. I. Hill, who is now the superintendent of the Nazarene work in the Barbados Islands. Our stay in Long Beach was very pleasant and our convention was owned and blessed of the Lord.

From Long Beach we had a long run; our next convention was in Newton, Kansas. We were from early Monday morning to Wednesday reaching Newton. It was held in the First Church of the Nazarene of which our good Brother A. L. Hipple was pastor. The reader will remember that A. L. Hipple and his good wife were in the big brown tent campaign. No finer people have ever lived than A. L. Hipple and beautiful Mabel. In all of my travels I have never seen a more beautiful Christian character than Sister Mabel. The dear Lord did not lend her to Brother Hipple and this country only for a few years until He took her unto Himself and today Sister Mabel is with her Lord.

The Newton convention made history. In that convention a fine young man, who worked in the railroad shops, and his wife were sanctified. This was our good Brother Mathis, who has just built and completed a great church in East Dan Diego. They were sanctified and Brother Mathis was called to preach. At the close of this convention, instead of going back to the shops, they boarded the train for our Nazarene college at Pasadena, California. He went to school for several years and became one of our leading pastors. He has built a very great church and work in East San Diego. At this writing he is just turning his church over to my old friend, Rev. Joseph Bates, and Brother Mathis is going to try the evangelistic field for awhile.

At the close of our convention at Newton our work had so piled up on us that the second time Brother Ruth had to divide the party, so he secured Brother and Sister Gouthey again and sent Brother Huff and the Goutheys to Mitchell, South Dakota, while Brothers Ruth, Robinson and the Wells went to Oklahoma City. We were there in the First Church of the Nazarene. One of my friends of nearly thirty years' standing, Rev. John Oliver, who is now District Superintendent of the Arkansas District, was their noble pastor. Our convention was one of interest and profit. So many of the friends came down from the college at Bethany and for many miles the autos were buzzing from every direction. The spirit of the convention was lovely. At the close we made a run for Blackwell, Oklahoma. There Brother Drake, who is at this writing our pastor in the First Church of the Nazarene in San Diego, was the good Nazarene pastor at that time. They secured the big city hall for our convention and he worked in connection with the Oklahoma Holiness Association. This was a wonderful convention. My, my, the people came from every quarter.

At the close of this great convention we made a run to Emporia, Kansas. Rev. C. E. Woodson, an elder in the Methodist Episcopal Church, and a young man whom I have known for more than thirty years, at that time was located in Emporia. I might just add that C.

E. Woodson was one of the young men that was put out of the great Southern Methodist Church on the same night that I was put out, so we have been friends for a long, long time. He had worked in connection with Dr. Wise, pastor of First Friends church, and with a fine Free Methodist pastor and they had put on this convention. Our convention was held in the Friends church of which Dr. Wise was pastor. Emporia at that time was the home of the noted Walt Mason, whose philosophy is published in hundreds of papers in the country, for everybody knows Uncle Walt. At the close of our convention Brother Ruth organized a splendid holiness association with C. E. Woodson as president with many fine assistants.

From Emporia we made a run to Decatur, Illinois. We were there with the First Church of the Nazarene. This was a very beautiful convention and a very profitable one. We had friends that came for two hundred and fifty miles to attend this convention.

At the close of this great convention we made a run down to Cairo, Illinois. I saw there a great catfish that was caught in the Mississippi river and brought into the market. His head was eighteen inches across and his great horns were nearly a foot long. He weighed nearly three hundred pounds. He was so big that his head looked like an ox's head. The reader will say that is a fish story. Exactly so. I am the man that saw the fish, but I am not the man that caught it.

From Cairo we made a run to Louisville, Kentucky, and opened our convention in the First Church of the Nazarene of which our good Brother Trumbauer was

pastor. Our convention took on such proportions that
our church would not accommodate the women, much
less the multitude, so we moved to the Christian and
Missionary Alliance tabernacle, that would seat about
one thousand people and had in connection a large
inquiry room where the seekers were taken and instructed. When I related my hospital experience, in
that one service we had between thirty and forty saved.
We enjoyed working with the saints in Louisville very
much. Almost every day we would have a little time
to run up to the Pentecostal Publishing Company and
talk with Brother Pritchard, the business manager.

From Louisville we made a trip up through the
beautiful bluegrass region over to the lovely little city
of Somerset. Our convention here was held in the
First Southern Methodist church. This was a large,
beautiful building, just completed. It was built by that
fine Brother Clark. He is the same man that built the
big Methodist church in Wilmore, Kentucky. He was
one of the first graduates of Asbury College, back in
the days of the famous Dr. John Hughes, who has been
one of the greatest sin-killers and devil drivers, that old
Kentucky has ever produced. Dr. John Hughes would
die before he would compromise a hair's breadth on
second blessing holiness. He has turned out many
great holiness preachers, and Brother Clark was one of
the first ones.

At the close of our great convention I ran over to
Wilmore, Kentucky, and gave them one night in the
college. This was a beautiful night. God was glorified,
the devil defeated and the kingdom of God was made

to flourish and prosper with the souls of a number of men and women.

Our next regular convention was at Indianapolis in one of the large Methodist churches. Brother Huff and Brother Gouthey had come across from the north and joined us in Indianapolis and we closed up the first coast-to-coast campaign on the last Sunday of April, 1920.

Here the band was broken up, Huff and Gouthey going north, Brother Ruth stopping over at home awhile, and Brother and Sister Wells and this old globe-trotter made a trip to the Southwest, stopping one night in Kansas City at First church and I stopped off two days in Emporia. The association that we organized when there a few months before had arranged for me to come back for two days. We gave one night to First Friends church and one night to First Free Methodist church.

From there I went down to Lyons and met Brother and Sister Wells there. Our stay in Lyons was very delightful. They had a large, beautiful tabernacle; splendid rooms in a good hotel; multiplied hundreds of people to preach to. Brother Thomas Keddie was the pastor in charge and this convention was supported by the good holiness people for miles around.

At the close of this camp Brother and Sister Wells took off a week or two to visit old friends in Kansas and Oklahoma, while this old soldier packed his grips and made a trip to Arlington, Texas, and was with Brother J. T. Upchurch at the great Berachah Home over the third Sunday of May, in their great anniver-

sary. This was a beautiful convention. I preached to
people by the hundreds and I suspect several thousands. The Berachah family had prayed the glory
down and we had people from all parts of Texas and
even Oklahoma. During our convention they had on a
great chautauqua in Arlington and they had such orators as William Jennings Bryan, and yet the people
said that the crowds at the great holiness convention
were several times as large as at the chautauqua.

After closing Sunday, on Monday morning I ran
down to Hubbard City, Texas, to visit my old mother
who was at that time eighty-seven years of age. I
spent two days with her. My little niece, Miss Eula
Kain Hammers, took mother and myself to visit a great
many of the beautiful old saints who listened to me
preach over forty years ago. In those days I was a
mere boy and they were middle-aged men and women.
When I went to see them many of them were from
seventy-five to ninety years of age. I will never forget
that little trip. My mother and I sang old hymns together in every home I went to, and I had prayers with
them and my mother and the old saints would shout
together. That little trip lingers with me yet. That
was the last time I ever looked on my beautiful, old
mother's face. The morning I left her, I will never
forget. Mother and I sang and quoted Scripture and
shouted together. After reading and praying together
and having a shouting spell I had to tell mother good-
by. Neither of us thought we would ever meet again
in this world. The last time I saw mother she was
standing in the yard waving her hand at me and shout-

ing just as loud as she could whoop. The next time that I see her will be at the great marriage supper of the Lamb.

My brother-in-law, Brother Henry King, took me to town and I boarded the old Cotton Belt and started for Chase, Kansas. I reached there on Friday before the fourth Sunday in May. There Brother and Sister Wells joined me. Our good Brother A. L. Hipple was the pastor in Chase at that time and our home was with him and beautiful Mabel. We had one of the best times of our life, for we had spent eighteen months together in that big brown tent campaign a few years before. When we met it was one old-fashioned shouting time. I will never forget how Sister Mabel and Sister Eunice ran into each other's arms and Brother Hipple and Kenneth got their arms around each other while I shouted for joy. At the close of our convention here we started north, stopping for one night in Kansas City, visiting the Publishing House and then making the run for Omaha, Nebraska. When we reached Omaha, Brother and Sister Wells went on to Shenandoah, Iowa, to visit his father and brothers, while I stayed for a three days' convention. I was called to this convention by Brother Will Fozier, a great business man, who is nothing short of a miracle of God's saving grace and healing power. At one time his face was nearly half eaten away and God healed him miraculously. I had three great days in his home and preached in a large, beautiful church, it seems to me that it was an Evangelical church. The singing was led by Miss Marie Danielson. I remember one night we had the altar pretty well lined up with Catholics and they were most gloriously saved, and the next night, I think, four of them were sanctified and united with that good pastor and his people.

Early Friday morning I was up and made a run to Oskaloosa, Iowa, to help in the campmeeting. The campmeeting that year was unusually interesting, from the fact that in the fall before Dr. C. J. Fowler, who had been president of the National Association for the Promotion of Holiness for twenty-five years, had been called to his reward, and as Brother Ruth was field secretary, he was the one that put on the coast-to-coast campaign. During this campmeeting a new president was to be elected, and we had the members of the National Association from a number of states, some from as far as New York and many from the central states. They had a great band of workers for that year and the annual meeting of the Association was in session three or four days. Rev. Will H. Huff was chosen as president of the National Association for the Promotion of Holiness. They had for their called workers that year Rev. C. H. Babcock, Rev. T. C. Henderson, Rev. A. P. Gouthey, Miss Minnie Lawhead, Miss Virginia Shaffer, Miss Stella McNutt and this writer, while the leading men of the Association were there to take part. Dr. John L. Brasher, who was president of Central Holiness University at that time, was elected president of the Iowa Holiness Association. From that convention they went out to all quarters of the nation. I have never seen more people taking trains and autos leaving one camp ground in my life than at the close of that great camp.

It had been arranged for Brother and Sister Wells and myself to go back to Shenandoah, Iowa, and give them a four days' convention. We opened in the First Methodist church on Monday night after the second Sunday of June. In four days we had one hundred and eighty people at the altar. This was the first holiness meeting that had been in that church for twenty years. Twenty years before they had said publicly that no holiness man could ever come into that pulpit and preach the second blessing. They went on with their religious activities, they may have paid their pastor and taken in a lot of members, but they had run twenty years without a revival of Holy Ghost heart-felt religion, but God at last sent them one.

The presiding elder prevailed on me to run out to Blanchard, where they were having the annual meeting of the Epworth League, with over two hundred in attendance. In the morning service we had seventy-five at the altar seeking holiness. They adjourned in the afternoon and came in a body to Shenandoah for the closing service that night. There is no way to tell just how many were at the altar but altogether in four days it ran to one hundred and eighty. I was offered by one of their leading men a hundred dollars a night to help him campaign for a month, but I was so tied up and booked that I knew it would be impossible to change my slate so I had to refuse.

From there Professor Wells and wife and this writer made a flying trip to Lincoln, Nebraska. We were there in what is known as the Epworth Park in that great campmeeting. My, my, but the crowds we preached to. While we were there Dr. E. T. Adams and Brother Will Yates came by and stayed with us a couple of days. Brother Adams brought one great message and Brother Yates did some great singing, also Brother Brasher had come from the university and was going to do some work in Nebraska and stayed two days with us. He brought us one of the greatest messages on the dangers of the human soul and the oncoming judgment day that I ever heard.

At the close of our great camp Brother and Sister Wells went back East, and this old globe-trotter made a trip to the West. I made a run down to a little railroad junction and there got the fast train from Omaha to Los Angeles by way of Salt Lake City. This was one of the longest and heaviest trains I ever made a trip on. There were two large locomotives, six baggage and mail cars, two dining cars and twelve Pullmans. Every berth was taken, upstairs and down. It is remarkable what the railroad companies have done. We came through those great mountains making from thirty-five to forty-five miles an hour with that heavy train and pulled into Los Angeles, California, on schedule time. In making that run from Omaha they never lost one minute.

CHAPTER XII

I reached home and had one day of rest and then took my family and little Sally and her tots and we made a run for the Southern California campmeeting, that is conducted by the Southern California Holiness Association at beautiful Santa Monica by the sea. Our workers that year were Rev. Joseph Smith, Rev. Will Kirby and Rev. Bud Robinson. We had a most beautiful camp out there. We ran over the Fourth of July and to say that we had people by the thousands is putting it tame. Oh, the good people that we saw saved and sanctified. We announced one day that the next morning from six to seven o'clock I would have a healing service. Beloved, by six o'clock the next morning the campmeeting was working alive with the people. I brought a short message and we began to anoint people and pray with them and they began to shout and that healing service ran until eight o'clock. There is no finer association to work for than the Southern California Holiness Association and no truer yoke-fellows to preach with than Brother Joseph and Will Kirby. This made the second camp that we had held together. The year before the same band of preachers held a campmeeting at Huntington Beach. There is nothing finer than the companionship, friendship and fellowship of preachers of the gospel. May God bless the memory of these two great men.

But how quick a campmeeting comes to an end when a tired preacher is camping on the banks of the ocean with his family. It was all too short, for at the close of this camp the Robinson family with the Welch grandbabies drove back into beautiful Pasadena. There I boarded the Southern Pacific and headed for Dalhart, Texas. My, my, but going through the deserts, talk about hot weather, it was well-nigh scalding. This meeting in Dalhart was arranged by our good Brother Lester Ketchum, who had been connected for a few years with the Pasadena College. My yoke-fellow in Dalhart was Rev. J. T. Upchurch, from the Berachah Home at Arlington, Texas, and his band of faithful workers were in charge of the music. To say that we had a good time is not half of it. Brother Jim would preach until his red head would almost strike fire and the Berachah Quartet would literally sing the heavens open. Our fellowship was beautiful and glorious.

But think of this, reader, and then pity an old, tired evangelist; in that hot, scorching weather I had to make a run from Dalhart, Texas, to Sale City, Georgia, away down near the Florida line. The campmeeting there had been established a few years before by that untiring worker, Rev. W. W. McCord. I have been in that campmeeting four times. It is no trouble to get crowds to preach to in Georgia in the summer time. We had them to peddle, by the hundreds and I judge by the thousands. I roomed in the home of Rev. W. W. McCord. He has a very large home and he filled it up with people. The workers and visitors made it their headquarters. Brother McCord hired two cooks and almost fed the campmeeting. He bought from twelve to fifteen large watermelons every morning and peaches and figs by the basket and chickens by the dozens, to feed the workers and visitors. My, my, what a time we had in that blessed old Southern home. The people are so clever and kind that it blesses you to just shake hands with them.

Now think of this run; I left Sale City for Chicago, Illinois. There our good Nazarenes had planned a big campmeeting in the suburbs of Chicago with such men as Schurman, Messenger, Jack Berry, Dave Anderson and Rev. C. H. Strong. The called workers were General Superintendent Williams and Dr. C. H. Babcock, Miss Virginia Shaffer and this writer, with Father Riggs from New England to hold the early morning prayermeetings. They had singers by the hundreds. Brother Schurman was the general manager of this great campmeeting. We had seekers until you could not keep up with the number. Thank the Lord for such campmeetings where the old-time gospel is preached in its purity and power with the Holy Ghost sent down from heaven.

I could only stay for one week in that great camp and my next run was to Conneautville, Pennsylvania. There I joined Rev. Will H. Huff and Rev. T. C. Henderson and Rev. A. P. Gouthey, with big Brother John Harris in charge of the music and Brother Jim Harris in charge of the camp as their general manager. This was the first and also the last time that I have ever visited that beautiful old camp ground. I was there

for only a week. The camp was established some thirty
years ago by that great man, Brother Hampe. The
camp is called Peniel, and is located at Conneautville,
Pennsylvania, on a beautiful lake. My stay was beautiful and the fellowship was sweet and complete.

While there Dr. and Sister Sloan were in a great
campmeeting at New Castle, Pennsylvania, and they
sent a man to Conneautville to take me to New Castle
in a car. This was a lovely trip down through that
beautiful old state. We arrived in time for the evening
service and it looked like everybody was trying to get
into that one night's service. It was a most beautiful
service.

At the close of the service, I made a run into Pittsburgh and there I got a train to Frankfort, Indiana, to
join battle with Dr. John W. Goodwin and Miss Virginia Shaffer in the campmeeting that was run by the
International Holiness Church. This was a great camp.
Brother Ewing is their District Superintendent and one
of the finest men that you will meet in a life-time's
travel. There were hundreds of fine workers, as their
District Assembly was to be held at the close of this
campmeeting. Their preachers and workers were there
from all over the state and from several other states.
They have a beautiful camp ground and a very large
tabernacle and a great dining room. Our fellowship
was beautiful and God gave us hundreds of precious
souls.

From this camp I ran over for one night to Kokomo
and there spoke in the First M. E. church to at least
fifteen hundred people.

The next night I ran down to Marion and gave them one night and the next day I ran down to Seymour to attend the District Assembly. This was a most wonderful assembly. Rev. J. W. Short was District Superintendent and Dr. R. T. Williams presided in the assembly. As our church there had just been burned down, the pastor of the First M. E. church offered his church for all day services and the City Park was used at night. Brother George Church, our good pastor, had our church near enough completed to feed the great crowds in the basement. That was one of the largest District Assemblies I ever attended. I preached at night from the grandstand to several thousand people. The people of that town said they had no idea that there were as many Nazarenes on earth as were in Seymour at that time.

From Seymour I ran down to Springer, Illinois, to the campmeeting. This camp was established by that good Dutchman, Jacob Flack, and the camp is called Jacob's Camp. My yoke-fellows were Brother George and Sister Effie Moore. May God bless her precious memory to the good of every person that she ever preached to. I went to the camp ground for six years.

At the close of this camp I went to Vincennes and joined my good friend, Callie Johnson, for a three days' convention and from there we went for one night to Bicknell and joined our good friend, Brother Hertenstein. We had a great night; got forty subscriptions for the Herald of Holiness and raised $1400 for the church and had nearly twenty saved in that one service.

From there I made a run to Akron, Ohio, and joined

Brother H. B. Macrory and had one of the best meetings, almost of my life.

From there I worked my way across the country
and joined Brother C. W. Ruth and Professor Kenneth
Wells and wife. I reached them on November 11, just
one year to a day after I had reached them the year
before. This time we opened in Brooklyn, New York,
in the Utica Avenue church. At that time Brother
William Howard Hoople was the pastor. The night
before I arrived they had prayed all night and by the
next day the glory was on until we could not preach.
This was a most wonderful convention; wave after
wave of glory would sweep the congregation until we
could not preach or hardly sing a song. Professor
Wells would start a song and the shouts would begin
again until you could not do anything but just let them
shout. Our home was with Brother Hoople. My, my,
but what a beautiful brother he was. He, like so many
others, has gone to live with Jesus.

At the close of this great convention we made a run
to Ashland, Kentucky. There we had a great convention and many precious souls were saved and sanctified.
Our stay in Ashland was one of delight.

From Ashland we made a run to Chicago and had
a great convention in the First Church of the Nazarene.
Here we were joined by Rev. John Norberry, from
Brooklyn. While we were in Brooklyn, Brother Ruth
had engaged him to travel with the party and we were
then together for four months. At Chicago we had one
of the finest conventions on the entire trip as Brother
Schurman has a very strong and a very spiritual

church. On the last day in the afternoon they put on a great missionary rally. The speakers were Sister Stella Crooks and Miss Lela Hargrove. The missionary offering amounted to several thousand dollars. One man gave a thousand dollars to foreign missions.

From Chicago we made a run to Akron, Ohio. In this convention Dr. Sloan and his men met in a great preachers' convention in connection with the coast-to-coast campaign. As we have already stated, Brother H. B. Macrory was the pastor. I have never been in a convention that was better entertained than the one in Akron. I don't think I ever saw so much good provisions brought in to feed the workers as we saw there, but with Dr. Sloan and Sister Sloan on the district and Brother Macrory as pastor they simply could do anything they wanted to do. We must have had at least fifty preachers in attendance.

From Akron we made a run to Detroit, Michigan. There we had a wonderful convention, though we had only about thirty Nazarenes in the city. The work had just been organized but there was more money given in the Detroit convention than in any other on the entire campaign. Rev. I. G. Martin had just been there and held a great revival and organized a Church of the Nazarene. Our convention was held in one of the largest halls in the heart of the city.

From Detroit we made a run to Dayton, Ohio. There we have a nice church; Brother Preston Roberts was the fine pastor and Brother E. E. Wordsworth was the District Superintendent of the Ohio District. We had people saved by the scores. Our District Superintendent was in charge of the preachers' convention and it was far-reaching. People from all over the state were there.

Our next convention was held in First Church of the Nazarene, Indianapolis. We ran over the holidays and had a great convention, three big services each day, Ruth, Norberry and Robinson doing the preaching, and the Wells doing the singing. This was a most wonderful convention. The cold wave struck us and my, my, but we shivered in the cold, but the people came in droves. Brother Ruth slipped and fell on the ice-covered sidewalk and almost broke his back and we had to leave him at home for over two weeks.

Norberry and Robinson and Professor and Sister Wells went on to St. Louis for the first convention of the new year. We held it in the Maplewood Church of the Nazarene. Our beloved Brother Cox was the fine pastor and we had a great convention. On Monday night after we closed we all went to the Flower Memorial church for a great rally and had a great service.

At midnight we left for Little Rock, Arkansas, and there the two Arkansas Districts, the Eastern Oklahoma District and the Louisiana District all, as far as they could, united in a great preachers' meeting and the coast-to-coast convention all in one. The city furnished us the large tabernacle and lit and fired it all at the expense of the city. We could not have had better crowds or better entertainment. Brother J. E. Moore, who was at that time in charge of one of the Arkansas Districts, was elected as the general manager of the entire convention. J. E. Moore is a gentleman of the first magnitude. He is now our pastor at the First Church of the Nazarene, Houston, Texas.

At the close of this great convention we made a run to Oklahoma City First Church of the Nazarene and were with my old friend, Rev. John Oliver, whom we were with a year before. Brother Ruth had so improved that he came on to Oklahoma City and joined us. We had a great convention.

From there we made a run to Sherman, Texas. We held our convention there in the First Southern Methodist church. Our good pastors, Brother and Sister Dillingham, had secured this great church for the convention and there we had another preachers' meeting in connection with the convention. They had secured General Superintendent Williams to preach every morning to the preachers. They came from all parts of the country. Sherman is a great Methodist school town and there were a great many fine, old, superannuated preachers there, many of them from seventy-five to eighty-five years of age. This convention was a great blessing to them. They said they had heard the greatest preacher in the nation. We had a most glorious time and never had better crowds. The great church was packed day and night.

From Sherman we made a run to Hamlin, Texas. Hamlin is on the Hamlin District and Rev. Allie Irick was their untiring District Superintendent. He brought his preachers from all parts of Western Texas. At that time Professor A. S. London was in charge of the Hamlin College. They had secured the First Southern Methodist church and we had there a great convention.

From Hamlin we made a long run west. We jumped from Hamlin, Texas, to Albuquerque, New Mexico. Our Hamlin meeting had grown so large that they wanted to run another week and so Brother John Norberry was left at Hamlin to run a week longer while the rest of the party went to New Mexico. We had a great convention at the First Southern Methodist church. Brother Lee Gaines was our Nazarene pastor and Brother Vanderpool was the Southern Methodist pastor. He opened up his large church and showed us all the kindness that a Christian gentleman could show a band of Christian workers of another church. At this writing Brother Lee Gaines is our splendid pastor at North Little Rock, Arkansas, and thank the Lord he is doing fine. At present Brother Vanderpool is the pastor of the First Southern Methodist Episcopal church at Holdenville, Oklahoma. I was in his church while touring Oklahoma in December, 1926, and the house was packed and a great service.

From Albuquerque we made a run to the First Church of the Nazarene at Phœnix, Arizona, and there we were joined again by Brother Norberry. We had a fine convention and enjoyed our old-time friends from Arkansas and Texas and also from Chicago. We were entertained by Brother Marvin and Sister Lillie Young and it was the limit for goodness. From Phœnix we made a run to Long Beach, California, and were there with Brother J. I. Hill, who is at this writing our superintendent in the Barbados islands. Our stay at Long Beach was a most delightful one. After working the inland states for a full year it was great to visit the old Pacific ocean again and see the blue breakers roll and splash and run out onto the sandbars and whoop and yell and pick themselves up and run back to the ocean and turn to saltwater again. We could not have enjoyed our stay more than we did.

At the close of the Long Beach convention we made a run to Ontario, California, and there had a most delightful convention. As many of my readers may know, Ontario is located in the great orange belt of Southern California, and of course everybody wanted to supply us with oranges off of their trees.

CHAPTER XIII

When this beautiful convention was closed Brother Norberry went back east to New York and Brother C. W. Ruth, Professor Wells and wife and this old soldier made a run to the north. Our first convention was at Portland, Oregon. At that time Brother Alpin Bowes was our pastor, but he secured the large Southern Methodist church for this convention and we had great crowds as the church was a very large one and at that time there was in the Oregon State Holiness Association at least one thousand members and with so many holiness people in the city it was easy to have a very large crowd. We were in Portland one year before going south, and this year we are going north.

Our next stop was in Seattle, with our good pastor, Brother McShane. We had a fine convention in Seattle having some services in the Free Methodist College and one service in the First Methodist Episcopal church, where one afternoon I gave my hospital experience to a very large crowd. We had in that one service nearly forty saved. The crowds came to the Nazarene church until just about half of them had to stand outside of the church.

At the close of this great convention we made a run to Walla Walla, Washington. I stopped off on Monday night and gave them one night at North Yakima. At that time Brother Will Nerry and his good wife were in charge at Yakima and we had one great night and on Tuesday I joined the rest of the party at Walla Walla. At that time Rev. U. E. Harding was their noble pastor. We had a great time in Walla Walla. As I had held a number of meetings there it insured us large crowds. Brother C. W. Ruth also had held a number of good meetings in Walla Walla, and our old friends and new ones came in droves so our convention was very large and a very beautiful gathering. From Walla Walla we made a long run, stopping at Greeley, Colorado, where my old friend of other days, Rev. C. H. Lancaster, was in charge, and our good District Superintendent Brother A. E. Sanner was with us. We had a most remarkable revival with the good people from all parts of that great Colorado country. Brother A. G. Crockett from Denver came up with a great band of his fine people and we had several carloads from Cheyenne, Wyoming, and from many other places. We had there a very remarkable experience. While the convention was going on we had a telegram from Dr. John L. Brasher, telling us that his son Paul was at the point of death, asking us to pray for his recovery. Brother C. W. Ruth read the telegram to the church and called them to prayer, and while we prayed the saints were so blessed that many shouted all over the church and every one of us felt that God had healed him, but God had done something better. His beautiful, blood-washed spirit had been translated. Some time after that I met Dr. Brasher and he told me that everybody that had prayed for Paul was so blessed that everyone thought he was healed. One of the poets wrote, "God moves in a mys-

terious way, His wonders to perform; He plants His
footsteps in the sea and rides upon the storm."

From Greeley we made another run on east, stopping at Burr Oak, Kansas. Here our good Brother
Dameron was in charge. My home was with Brother
John Korb. We had in Burr Oak one of the finest
meetings that we probably had on the entire campaign.
People, people! My, my, how they came to that convention. To say hundreds is putting it tame; the
crowds were so large that many of the good people
would take their lunches and after the afternoon service
they would stay there in the church until the night
service for fear that they could not get room at night.

After this good time with the saints we had to make
another run to the east and our next stop was with
Rev. William E. Fisher, pastor of the First Church of
the Nazarene, Kansas City, Missouri. At that time
Professor Ben Sutton and his beautiful little wife, Sister Margie, were in charge of the music and were assistants to Brother Fisher. This convention was much
longer than most of the conventions. We opened on
Tuesday night and ran through two Sundays. As a
rule we only ran over one Sunday, but all hands felt
that in that city at our headquarters we ought to stay
longer than a week. We had very large crowds. I
have often seen every seat up and downstairs taken
and then extra seats brought in and then all the standing room taken. We had there, I judge, the finest
singing that we had on the entire trip, as the Wells
children and Brother Ben and Sister Margie were all
great singers, and the four together almost lifted the

roof from the big church. I don't think I have ever
heard four gospel singers that sang better together than
the Wells and the Suttons. While in the great city we
had the privilege of visiting the Publishing House almost every day. One day at noon we dropped in on
the boys and they were praying a fellow through at
their noon prayermeeting and then I wrote these lines
on the Publishing House:

> I found by observation
> That our house of publication,
> Keeps up its reputation
> As a soul salvation station;
> And as a bureau of information
> On the line of full salvation
> It is the fairest in the nation
> Or in all God's creation.

Our stay at headquarters was of much interest to us
boys on the field.

From Kansas City we made a run to Kearney, Nebraska. There Sister Wheeler, the noble pastor, had
everything in fine shape, and our good District Superintendent, Brother Ludwig, and his good wife were
with us in the convention. We had a most glorious
time in Kearney. At the close of this campaign, Brother and Sister Wells left us to go into their campmeeting
work.

Brother Ruth and I made a run to Mitchell, South
Dakota. Our old friends, Brother and Sister Brandy-
berry, were in charge and there we had a great convention in the courthouse, or perhaps it was in the city
hall, but we had plenty of people and a great revival.
At the close of our Mitchell campaign our coast-to-

coast party was brought to an end. Brother Ruth and I left Mitchell together and ran down to Sioux City, Iowa, and changed cars for Chicago, reaching there the next morning in time for breakfast. We transferred across the great city, I to go east and Brother Ruth south. I was headed for Cleveland and Brother Ruth for Indianapolis. We separated at the station. We had then finished two years of coast-to-coast work. It was hard for us to separate. We stood and looked at each other and then put our arms around each other and wept like children and promised each other to stand true to the doctrine and experience of entire sanctification as a second work of grace until we met each other on the shores of eternal deliverance.

I believe we have never had a finer leader in the holiness movement than Brother C. W. Ruth. He can plán and hold more holiness conventions than any man in the great holiness movement and have the best revivals in these great conventions. I have worked with almost all the holiness boys in the United States and no man ever yoked up with a truer yoke-fellow than Brother C. W. Ruth.

I found in Chicago that the regular trains would not get me to Cleveland in time to preach that night but I also found that I could pay five dollars extra and take that fast train from Chicago to New York which made only two stops between Chicago and Cleveland. We ran into Cleveland that night in time to open up in the big tabernacle. I was met at the station by Brother C. Warren Jones and in a short time we were in the Nazarene parsonage, which is about as near heaven as any place on earth. There is nothing finer above dirt than the home of a good Nazarene preacher. My, my, but they are the sacks of salt for the hungry sheep to lick at. Brother Jones had everything in fine shape and the meeting was well advertised. Brother Jones had secured the student body from the Friends Bible School to have charge of the music. Sometimes as many as a hundred would be on hand. We also had the famous colored quartet. They were great singers.

From Cleveland I made a run with Brother and Sister Jones and their delegates to Pittsburgh to the District Assembly. This was a beautiful trip, from Cleveland to Pittsburgh. The Nazarenes were there from every quarter. Good Dr. Sloan, District Superintendent, with Brother Reynolds, General Superintendent, had the work well in hand and everything was beautiful. I stayed with them three days, preaching two nights.

From Pittsburgh I made a run to the campmeeting at Olivet, Illinois. We had one of the best camps that had ever been held on the grounds up to that time. This was one great camp; people there by the thousands and hundreds were at the altar.

From there I started west. I stopped one night about the first of June at Wray, Colorado, with my good friend and brother, L. E. Grattan. At that time Brother E. Arthur Lewis was out on the plains, some twenty miles away, but they dismissed their crowds and came by several automobile loads. He sang that night one of his famous songs, "When the Old Man Died."

From Wray, I ran over for one night in Colorado Springs. Here a good brother, Jim Black, was in charge. We had a fine service.

I left there with Brother A. E. Sanner, our good District Superintendent. We made a run from there to Florence, Colorado, and preached in the afternoon. While we were there preaching a great rain came and we made a run up the valley to Canyon City, but it rained so hard there that for three days we could scarcely get to church and I could not get out of the town. It was on this night, June 3, of the awful storm that flooded the Royal Gorge, overflowing the Arkansas river and destroying Pueblo, Colorado, where hundreds of homes were swept away. The big depot was destroyed, one passenger train washed away and hundreds of freight cars, some of them washed ten miles down the river.

Leaving Canyon City I ran over to Grand Junction and stayed three days with a good Nazarene pastor. Leaving Grand Junction I made a hot trip across the desert back to Los Angeles in time to take in the campmeeting at the Palisades. The workers that year were Rev. Joseph Smith, Rev. Fred Ross, and this writer. The Lord gave us a most beautiful campmeeting.

I then made a trip back east holding a number of campmeetings, visiting Wilmore, Kentucky; Camp Sychar, Ohio; Romeo, Michigan; back through Dayton with a chain of short conventions through northern Indiana; through Kansas City and on to Henryetta, Oklahoma, reaching there for the District Assembly. As my friends may know, Henryetta is in the East-

ern Oklahoma District. Our beloved Brother Mark
Whitney was District Superintendent and was re-
elected by a unanimous vote. Dr. John Goodwin
presided in this great assembly. The Eastern Oklahoma District that year had the largest increase of
membership and more churches organized than I had
ever known up to that time. Rev. M. B. Jobe was
pastor at Henryetta. As many people know, Brother
Jobe is one of the finest pastors in our great connection.
At this writing he is pastor of the First church at Walla
Walla, Washington. Jobe is a wonderful man because
he comes from the wonder state, Arkansas.

There have been more bad things said about Arkansas and there are more good things connected with
it than any other state in this nation. More good
preachers have come out of one community in Arkansas
than any place I have ever known. Our late Will
Dallas was from that part of the state; President N.
W. Sanford of Hutchinson, Kansas; Rev. Joseph N.
Speakes, District Superintendent of the Northwest District; Rev. B. H. Haynie, pastor of First church in
Akron, Ohio; Rev. J. E. Moore, pastor of First church
in Houston, Texas; Rev. G. E. Waddell, pastor of First
church in Cambridge, Massachusetts; Brother Harmon, pastor of First church of Henryetta, Oklahoma;
his brother, pastor of First church at Lufkin, Texas;
and Brother Sharpe, who has been a great pastor and
District Superintendent. At the present time there are
a number of the finest young pastors in Arkansas who
have gone out from that community. I might add that
Arkansas has the most beautiful mountains and the

largest cotton farms and largest peach orchards, has
the largest rice fields, has more mineral springs and
health resorts, and the only diamond field in the United
States is located in Arkansas.

But you must forgive me for this little detour. We
are back in the great District Assembly in Henryetta.
My home was with Brother C. P. Curry, the Southern
Methodist pastor, a good friend of mine of twenty
years' standing. Our convention was a great one. It
was during this convention that my mother went to
heaven. The night mother went up from Hubbard,
Texas, to the New Jerusalem, someone said to mother,
"Grandma, you are very feeble; shall we send for Buddie?" Mother said, "Why, children, don't you know
Buddie is in a meeting and what if he should come to
see me go up to get my crown and a dozen souls should
be lost?" That night while I preached my heart was
overflowing and there were a dozen men out of the oil
fields, who had been wild and reckless and God's Spirit
gave them a touch and a dozen of them wept their way
to the altar and just before midnight we had prayed
the last one through. An hour later I received a long
distance call that mother had gone to heaven. I notified them to put mother away nice and beautiful and
in a week or two I would come down and take care of
the expenses. The next day I walked the streets of
Henryetta and laughed and cried. I laughed because
mother had received her crown and I wept because I
was an orphan boy.

At the close of the meeting in Henryetta I ran down
to Allen, Oklahoma, and gave a week's convention,

closing on Sunday in the afternoon and made a run across to the beautiful little city of Ada, Oklahoma, and preached Sunday night. I then got a train out that night that got me next morning into Dallas, Texas. I made my way out from there to Hubbard City, Texas, where I spent a couple of days with my brothers and one sister. They and their families took care of my mother's last expenses. The reader will remember that a few pages back I described my last visit with my mother and how she stood in the yard and shouted. On the last trip to Hubbard City I could not bear to even go to the cemetery, for I knew mother was not there. I left Hubbard City, headed for the City in the skies.

I made a long trip to Sioux City, Iowa, where Rev. C. K. Spell was our splendid pastor. We had a ten days' meeting in which he raised me more money than was ever paid to me for one ten days' meeting in my life. If you want to hunt up somebody that is good, go and look at C. K. Spell, and to know Sister Annie and the children will bless you as long as you live. At the close of my meeting in the Nazarene church I gave a three days' meeting in the city to the Holiness Association. At that time my beloved Brother Will Hahn and his good sister Barbara were the leading workers in the mission. We had a glorious time in that old mission.

From there I made a run to Minneapolis, Minnesota. This was in November as you will remember. I reached there in a great snowstorm; the wind was so cold that it seemed to me that it would shave a man without the use of lather or a razor. Rev. E. E. Wordsworth was the pastor of that church. In the spring before Dr. John Goodwin and E. E. Wordsworth, with a few faithful workers, such as Ben Mathisen and his good wife, opened up a new work in Minneapolis. They bought the large German Methodist church and organized with some thirty-five members about the first of May. By November they had sixty-five. Brother Wordsworth had secured for the singers Brothers Kim and Nilan of Chicago. Brother Kim was born and reared in Denmark and Brother Nilan in Norway. Our good Brother Wordsworth was born in England; we took our meals with Brother Anderson who was born in Sweden, and my people had come over from Ireland. So in this meeting we had five nationalities represented as workers, England, Ireland, Sweden, Norway and Denmark. At that time there was a great deal of talk in the public press about a league of nations. In this meeting these five nationalities stood on the platform and locked arms and showed the congregation that holiness would solve the league of nations. As we had five nationalities represented in our band of workers we had people there from almost every country in Europe. I have never seen a much better meeting held in my life. Kim and Nilan had their musical instruments and such playing and singing you will scarcely hear in a lifetime, and the people came until there was no end to it. I remember one good brother in that city was not at all friendly to the organization of a Nazarene church, but when he saw they were going to organize anyway he said, "Oh, well, let them go on, nobody will come when they are organized." I remember we opened on Thursday night about the middle of November and by Sunday not half of the crowd could get into the church. This good brother came and waded around in the snow knee-deep for awhile and finally had to leave. He could not even push his way into the vestibule for the crowds. In spite of the prophecy of some good men concerning the Nazarene movement it is still moving. I think at the close of our convention we had almost a hundred members in the Church of the Nazarene.

I left Minneapolis headed for the Northwest. I made a run to Spokane, Washington, for a three days' convention with that beautiful young man, Weaver Hess. We had a tremendous crowd. On the second day we got up early in the morning and went away down to the city of Colfax, where they were having a district Sunday school convention. I preached in the morning for them. We had a nice lunch at noon; I went to preaching again at one, finished up at two, and at two-thirty we were headed again for Spokane. When we reached Spokane good Sister Hess had secured about three dozen of that little fish called the smelt and had us a great fish supper. My, my, but it was great and our convention was one of delight.

I made a run from there to Everett, Washington, where I preached in the old holiness tabernacle. We had a tremendous time. On Sunday morning I preached in the Nazarene church. Brother E. G. Anderson had just sent out word for all the churches to take an offering for foreign missions on the first Sunday of December. Our little church thought they could raise fifty dollars but two or three people had been sanctified in the meeting who were well-to-do and they all went down to the Nazarene church on Sunday morning. I asked how many people would give ten dollars and pretty soon it ran to one hundred dollars and some gave smaller gifts and brought it up to one hundred and fifty dollars in cash. In the afternoon I was to give my hospital experience. There were people from Snohomish, Bellingham and Seattle, Washington. We had a tremendous time and a great service. In that Everett convention I met an old friend whom I had not met for fifteen years, Brother Newberry, whom I used to work with in Virginia. He moved into New York about the time I moved to California and went with the Christian and Missionary Alliance and I had gone to the Church of the Nazarene. He brought his family and attended the convention in Everett.

I went from Everett to Seattle and there I was met at the train by Brother Newberry and he ran me over by the Nazarene parsonage. There Brother McShane gave me the slate that had been made out by himself and the Holiness Association. I was to go with Brother Newberry to Alliance Bible School and take dinner; he was to take me to the Greenlake Free Methodist church for the afternoon service. At that time Brother A. P. Gouthey was holding a convention in that church. We had a large crowd and a most interesting service. That night I was to preach in the Bible school. I have never had a much better service than I had that night in the

Bible school. The auditorium was packed to over-flowing. That night Brother Newberry was to take me to the home of Brother McShane and I spent the night or a part of it in the Nazarene parsonage. The next morning all hands of us were to go to the Free Methodist College for a morning service. At the close of this service we were to go to the home of Brother A. P. Gouthey for dinner, so the band of workers all went, and my, my, what a dinner that old boy had gotten up! Brother Gouthey knows how to do the thing. There was everything in Seattle that is good to select from. When dinner was over we hurried back to the Nazarene church where I preached in the afternoon and night. No more could get in the building and we didn't have room at the altar for any more. They came in droves. The next morning Brother Newberry came for me in his beautiful new Essex car and drove me down through that great highway and that lovely forest to Tacoma, Washington. There I had a two days' convention in the Church of the Nazarene with Brother and Sister Burns. Many of my old friends had attended the services in Seattle; Brother H. D. Brown and wife, and Brother Charles Rose and wife from Texas. Several car loads of them came down to Tacoma and gave us a boost there.

From there we made a run to Portland, Oregon. We had a three days' convention in the Nazarene church with Brother Bowes. I ran from there to Newberg, Oregon, and gave them an afternoon and night. I was there with that good Brother Pounds. He is one great boy. From Newberg I ran over to Salem and gave an afternoon and night with our good Brother Wells. We had lots of people saved in each one of these one day conventions.

Down the coast I go, stopping for a day and night with Brother Russell Gray in Berkeley, California. I reached home for Christmas as tired as a preacher could be but as happy as a bald-headed bumblebee in a hundred acres of red-top clover. This finished up the entire trip for 1921.

CHAPTER XIV

After the Christmas holidays were all enjoyed, the first of January, 1922, I went to Alhambra to hold a meeting for Brother Howard Eckel. This was a beautiful convention and many people were saved in the ten days. Brother Will Eckel and wife had come home from Japan. They gave us a great missionary rally, one of the most beautiful missionary services that I had ever seen. There is no finer man on earth to work for than Brother Howard Eckel.

When we finished up in Alhambra I made a run down to Whittier, California, with that greatest of pastors, C. W. Griffin. This was a great convention. We had our church packed to overflowing. We desired to secure a larger place but none was available. Brother Joseph E. Bates came down from Pasadena and we put on a special service and marched to a beautiful lot and broke dirt for the new church. So the reader can see that we made history in that convention. Many precious souls were saved.

From Whittier I went back to Los Angeles. I was there for three Sundays with one of the greatest old boys that is now living, that cultured gentleman, Dr. A. O. Henricks, who at this writing is president of Trevecca College, Nashville, Tennessee.

From Los Angeles I made a trip down that beautiful valley to the beautiful little city of Escondido. At that time my old friend and brother, Metcalf, was the pastor. We had many remarkable things to take place in that meeting. I referred to praying with a dying Christian Scientist and a lady jumped up and said, "I see now that a man can profess holiness and lie at the same time." "For," she said, "Christian Scientists don't die." I told her that it was very strange, for they took the man out and buried him and I couldn't believe an undertaker would knowingly take and bury a live man. She walked out of the church and said she would never darken that door again. But the next morning she came to the parsonage and brought a couple of fine Belgium hares dressed nicely for a love offering to the Nazarene pastor and family and the evangelist. She met us at the church that afternoon and got up publicly and begged pardon and came to the mourner's bench. She did some good digging. We prayed loud and long; she wiped the tears off her face and said she knew that God had saved her.

The little valley in which Escondido is located is about thirty miles back from the ocean and thirty miles northeast of San Diego. They tell me that Escondido means hidden valley. This valley is as near full of the white Leghorn chickens as I have ever seen anywhere on the face of the earth. You can go up on one little point in the city, a pretty little round hill, and look over the valley and count between forty and fifty great chicken farms. This is a very interesting place.

I came home from Escondido and rested up for two or three days, then ran into Los Angeles for the all-day meeting where Brother Fred Ross was holding meetings

in the Euclid Avenue Methodist Episcopal church. I
went from there to Elysian Heights and stayed two
days with good Brother Matthews, who has built the
big church in East San Diego. From there I ran down
to beautiful Santa Ana. There I had a beautiful meeting with my old friend, H. L. Humphreys. We had a
glorious meeting there. We had a good time and God
gave us a splendid revival.

From Santa Ana I went down to Cucamonga and
joined Brother E. M. Hutchens. The Lord gave us a
beautiful meeting in Cucamonga. We put on a great
drive there for the Sunday school. We agreed to give
every boy a nickel that would come to school with his
overalls on and bring some other boy with him. We
called it the overall brigade and my, my, the boys that
piled into that church. We had a most beautiful revival
and a number of converts, who desired to be baptized
by immersion. We had the baptismal service in the
church in Upland where we have a nice bapistry. We
went over one afternoon to baptize our converts, I
think it was our last Sunday of the meeting, the third
Sunday of April. At the close of our baptismal service
a number of ladies from one of the big churches in town
came to Brother Hutchens and said, "We have been
wanting to be immersed and our pastor did not believe
in it. Will you baptize us by immersion?" He said,
"Sure I will." He got ready and baptized as many
Methodists as Nazarenes.

At the close of this convention I came home for a
few days' rest and went to Glendora with a band of our
schoolboys who were holding a campmeeting. We had

a glorious time there and saw people saved at a regular mourner's bench in the beautiful little city of Glendora, where some people said a revival could never be held; but, beloved, God can save people anywhere in the world when they get through and want Him. It was wonderful how God worked in these meetings. If we put on a tent meeting in Southern California, especially in a town where we have no Nazarene church, it is anything but an easy job; it is a proposition of a lifetime. Nevertheless, our boys can do the job. There is no band of boys that is harder to defeat than a band of red-hot Nazarenes; in fact, they never know when they are defeated. That is one thing in a man's favor who doesn't know so much about this old world. When a man is bound to this old world it seems he is blind in one eye and deaf in one ear, therefore it takes spiritual dynamite to open his blind eye and unstop his deaf ear; but, thank God, He is ready for the emergency.

Leaving California the first of May, 1922, we had a chain of short conventions across the country reaching the campmeeting at the Olivet College about the last of May. That year Dr. John Matthews and the writer were the engaged preachers. We had a great many fine singers on the ground connected at that time with the college. At the close of this great Olivet Camp I worked through Ohio, putting in ten days at the great Sebring Camp. Then back as far north as Red Rock, Minnesota, through Romeo, Michigan, to Pontiac, and then a trip into the northern part of Michigan to the beautiful town of Selkirk, in a little Quaker church where we had a powerful convention.

From there back by Cleveland and a little later, after making a few short stops across Ohio, I joined Brother C. R. Chilton, District Superintendent of the Ohio District. Here we made twenty-five towns in a month. We were in Cincinnati over the great Thanksgiving day, where we fed several thousand children and had a great feed for the men at old George Street Mission at night. At that time Brother Lew Standley was in charge of the mission with his two beautiful daughters, Misses Ruth and Lily. The precious little girls were the most untiring workers I have ever known.

From Cincinnati I worked my way across the country, reaching home for Christmas. The first of January, 1923, Brother Harry Wenger, who is choir leader of First church, Pasadena, at this time went with me to Phœnix, Arizona, and we joined E. G. Roberts in a great campaign. This was one great meeting. At night there would not be one vacant seat or any standing room left.

At the close of this campaign Brother Wenger came back to Pasadena to school and I boarded the train for Miami, Florida. My, my, but this was a long run. Rev. I. G. Martin, who had been appointed District Superintendent of Florida, had put on a great tent campaign in Miami. Our beloved Brother Roby was the pastor and the church board had secured Brother Charles D. Tillman for the song leader and his daughter Jewel for the pianist. They had put in two pianos and Brother John Harris' wife was selected to play one and Jewel the other. Our campaign ran here for over a month. We had multiplied hundreds at the altar and during the month preached to people by the thousands. Dr. H. C. Morrison, editor of the Pentecostal Herald, also president of Asbury College, was there taking his rest in Miami at that time. He brought us some very great messages. We had with us in the meeting all the time Brother and Sister Huffman from Philadelphia, Brother and Sister Strong from Detroit, and Brother W. P. B. Kinert, from Epworth, South Carolina. All of these workers brought messages during this great campaign. They had a fine delegation of good holiness preachers come down from North Carolina and as Miami was full of tourists at that time we had people from all over the nation.

At the close of the campaign at Miami I ran up the coast one hundred and twenty-five miles to Fort Pierce. There I was met in an auto by two fine old boys who had come across nearly a hundred miles from Sebring, Florida. Brother Orville Sebring had been down a few days in Miami and engaged me to preach a few days in the Methodist church. This trip was a whole day's run, but we drove into Sebring in time for supper. I had three or four days that were beautiful. I ran across from Sebring and stopped a night in Waycross, Georgia, and preached in the Southern Methodist church.

From Waycross I ran across to Birmingham and preached two days for the Wesleyan Methodist boys. Brother Robert French was in charge. We had two great days. I went from there to Jasper, Alabama, and gave them two days in the Nazarene church. We had a glorious good time there with Brother Hooker and

Brother Lancaster. From there I went to Florence, Alabama, and gave them a couple of days. I went out and looked at the great Wilson dam and saw many interesting things about Florence.

I ran from Florence to Nashville and gave them a day at the school and from there I ran across to Wilmore, Kentucky, and gave them two days in Wilmore. From Wilmore I ran over to Louisville for a day with the Nazarene boys. From there I ran to Upland, Indiana, and was with Dr. John Paul three days at the Taylor University.

I ran from Upland back into Ohio and joined Brother C. R. Chilton again and during the month of March we made over twenty-five towns again. We literally worked Ohio like working a field. We preached to people by the multiplied thousands. I closed with him on the last Sunday of March. I came across from Ironton through Columbus, on across to Akron and was with Brother Macrory for one night and then went over and gave Brother Mattox a day and night in Warren, Ohio.

From there I made a run to Jackson, Michigan, with Brother Bush, our good pastor. I was with him Wednesday, Thursday and Friday and had a glorious good time, and on Saturday, the last day of March, I ran into Detroit. There I joined battle with Miss Essie Morris of Springfield, Tennessee, as song leader. My old friend, Marvin Cooper, was their fine pastor, and Brother Guy Nelson was chairman of the board.

Here is a little piece of history. The first meeting I ever held for Brother Joe McClurkan, Brothers Guy

Nelson, Marvin Cooper and Miss Essie Morris were all three sanctified in the same service, and behold, when I reached Detroit the first day of April, 1923, the three young people who were sanctified in the same service at Nashville, were now yoked up in a great battle for full salvation in Detroit. We had fifteen days that were beyond description for seekers and crowds.

I ran from there to Cleveland, Ohio, and I gave our good Brother Butler, president of Friends College, two days and nights in the Bible College. I also gave Brother C. Warren Jones two days and nights. I ran from there to the Chicago Central District and joined Brother E. O. Chalfant, and for the last ten days of April and all of May he and I toured that great district. I have a beautiful letter from him before me, telling all the places that we had toured. It might be a little tiresome for the reader to undertake to visit all these places for we made thirty towns in Illinois, winding up about May 21, at the great Olivet Camp. But in his letter he states that out of this campaign sixty Nazarene churches have been organized. That one campaign had added to the church property a quarter of a million dollars. We also raised money to buy twenty gospel tents. Under these tents during the summer season between eighty and ninety great tent campaigns were put on, running a month at a place. There were hundreds of thousands of people preached to under these tents during the four months of the summer season. Brother Chalfant says that he is very largely indebted to Uncle Buddie for helping to put this great district to the front; that he never could have done it without the assistance I gave him. We put the Herald of Holiness in hundreds of homes. Through that campaign he received hundreds of calls for meetings. He usually had from three to four good workers with each tent, which as the reader would see gave him a band of workers numbering seventy or eighty. These tents ran from the last of May until the last of September. At their District Assembly in September his report that was published in the Herald of Holiness was the greatest that had ever been for one year's time.

At the close of the Olivet Camp I boarded the train for the south. Stopped one night in Kansas City; went on to Oklahoma City and was met by Brother Stephen White who was president of Bethany-Peniel College. He took me out to Bethany and I preached in the afternoon and at night. We had great crowds and a glorious time. After preaching at night he ran me back to the city and at midnight I left for Fort Worth, Texas.

Here I joined Brother Mayfield, the head of the great Union Mission. I was with him for ten days. The Upchurch band of workers from the Berachah Home had charge of the music. There is no way to tell how much good a campaign like that did for Fort Worth. We had our buildings packed until the people stood up along the wall. At the close of the convention there I boarded the train for Pasadena, California. After having only two days' rest I took my family and we went out to the Pacific Palisades to the great camp-meeting. We ran through there and closed on July 8, coming in home that night.

On Monday of July 9, my wife and daughter Ruby

and the Rev. George C. Wise and this old globe-trotter left Pasadena headed for the Yellowstone National Park, but we had plenty of time so we ran to the ranch where my children lived at Rich Grove, California, and stayed a couple of days, then to Fresno, California, and took the Blackstone Trail into the Yosemite Valley. We drove in that night a few miles from the Mariposa woods. We spent the night in the Fish Lodge. This was a beautiful camp built of big logs. We were up early the next morning and drove up to the big forest before we had breakfast. These were the largest trees that I had ever seen up to that time. The largest one in that forest is known as Grizzly Giant, nearly three hundred feet tall, and thirty-two feet through. There were hundreds of other trees almost as large. It is in that forest that a highway is cut through one of the trees. We drove through this great tree and had our pictures made. There was one log that had fallen down and looked like the top had broken off and disappeared. This log was some two hundred feet long and the highway built along the side of it. It was nearly three times as high as our automobile top. There is one log, however, near the old Clark cabin that twenty-four horses have stood on at one time and had their pictures made. We had breakfast at the Montana. The reader will remember that these big trees are named for the different states and the Montana is a tree that is about twenty-eight feet through and nearly three hundred feet high. They have scaffolds up twenty or thirty feet and have built a big dining room out of logs and heavy lumber. It is very interesting. The big kitchen is off to one side and great heavy flooring nearly twenty feet long is laid on the great platform and runs endways up to the big tree and in a circle until they go clear round the tree; then the big banisters are put around and great logs stood on ends around the tree where they have laid heavy plates running to the corner post and that great circle is covered and makes a very unique dining room. After breakfast we went to Yosemite Valley and spent a couple of days. They claim the highest falls in the world are in this valley. There is one river that leaps out of the clouds and falls 1730 feet. Our two days were very delightfully spent in the Yosemite Valley. Horseback riding and hunting and fishing were the order of the day.

When we left the valley we made a run to Sacramento and joined Brother E. E. Mieras, our good pastor, and preached with him for one full week; from there we ran to Oakland and joined Brother Ralph Gray and gave him a week. Leaving Oakland we ran back to Sacramento in time for dinner. Brother Mieras' folks had planned a great chicken dinner and many of the good friends ran in. After dinner we made a run to Gridley. There Hunter and Martin were in a great tent meeting and we stayed and preached for them two nights.

When we left there we headed for the north, going through northern California and stopping at Shasta Springs and the great mountain, driving on through and putting up in good hotels at night. Finally, passing through northern California and beautiful old Oregon we reached Portland. There we stopped for dinner.

That afternoon we made the trip over the Columbia River highway, said to be the most beautiful highway in the world; in fact, I don't see how it could be surpassed for beauty and grandeur. The highway follows the great Columbia river for more than a hundred miles. We pulled into the beautiful little city of Nampa, and stopped to rest a few days with our friends, but of course preached over Sunday at the Nazarene church and went up and preached one night in Boise and had a glorious good time.

We left there for the Yellowstone National Park. We drove into the park on Wednesday after the first Sunday of August. Went in from the west gate. Here we saw such sights and wonders that it would take a whole history itself to describe the Yellowstone Park. The great paint pots, and boiling lakes, and mammoth boiling springs, growling, roaring geysers, roaring mountains, herds of bears, great herds of elks and buffaloes, groundhogs enough to give everybody in the world two apiece it looked like, the great Yellowstone lake and the Grand Canyon of the Yellowstone, a trip over Mt. Washburn, 10,000 feet high, spending one night at Old Faithful Inn, one night at Yellowstone lake, and two nights at the great Mammoth Hot Springs. We were in the park altogether five days and nights. I don't suppose any man living has been able to describe the wonders of Yellowstone National Park. It will pay any man on earth that can spare the time and money to spend a week in Yellowstone Park.

Leaving the park we had a nice long trip back across the mountains and plains of Idaho and stopped

again in Nampa, resting up two or three days, making
one little fishing trip and preaching one night in Meridian. Leaving Nampa we now headed back for the
south; stopped off in Portland and preached on Sunday
with Brother D. Rand Pierce, who was then pastor;
working our way back through Oregon, preaching a
few nights in Ashland, driving south through the great
peach, plum and prune orchards, fields of canteloupes,
watermelons and grapes until it looked like there was
no end to it; reaching Rich Grove, California, again
and spending a few days with our children.

Wife and Ruby and Mr. Wise came back to Pasadena but I stayed in Northern California District,
giving the boys a boost. A couple of days in Bakers-
field and a couple of days in Merced, going up to
Fresno and Stockton, then to beautiful Santa Rosa, the
home of the great Burbank, the plant wizard. I saw
things that he had produced that look impossible, yet
they were there to behold. From Santa Rosa I came
down the coast by Frisco and down to beautiful San
Jose. I gave three days there and closing on Sunday
night at midnight I boarded a fast train for Kansas
City, Missouri. Made the run from San Jose to Kansas City and was there for the opening of our great
General Assembly, which already has been written up
in a way that is impossible for me to do. However, we
had hundreds of as beautiful people as live on earth.

CHAPTER XV

At the close of the General Assembly, which was October 2, I joined Brother E. O. Chalfant and we made a run from Kansas City to Stockton, Illinois. From there to Martintown, Wisconsin, then to Baraboo. From there we went across to Minneapolis and joined Brother Wordsworth over Saturday and Sunday; leaving Minneapolis we came back to the beautiful little town of Menomonie, and made a run ten miles into the country where we have a nice country church. Had a great service with our good pastor, Brother Waltz, then back to Menomonie, got a train and went about a hundred miles; got off the railroad early next morning and went five miles in the country to a beautiful Quaker church and had a beautiful morning and afternoon service. That night we ran twenty miles and took several auto loads to Beulah camp grounds, where there is a large Methodist church, and had a great service. During the day I put the Herald of Holiness in eighty homes. The offering came up beautifully. That night we drove twenty-five miles to Richland Center and spent a part of the night with some good Kentucky friends. At break of day we boarded the train and pulled to Madison, Wisconsin, and had a good morning service and raised money to help take care of the pastor of a new church that had just been organized. That afternoon we ran into Racine; there I was joined by the Aeolian Quartet and held a week's convention for Oscar Hudson.

At the close of this convention we set in again and toured the most of Illinois, one night at a place. My, my, such trips as we had. We went to at least a dozen new churches that had just been organized since we left in May, giving each one a great boost. In some of them we raised as much as $1,000 to help put them across.

Coming back up to Chicago I gave Brother C. H. Strong a two Sunday meeting in the Austin church. This was a beautiful campaign. There is no finer man living to work for than Brother Strong. At the close of this convention I went over to Woodlawn church and gave Brother Haynie two Sundays. There on Monday, I was joined by good Brother Jarrette and Sister Aycock and we had one week together and they stayed for a week longer. Then I ran to St. Louis and gave my old friend, William E. Fisher, a beautiful campaign. Ran across and gave Kansas City one night. From there to Yuma, Colorado, and gave Brother Howard Eckel ten days. Ran over to Denver and gave Brother Crockett one night. From Denver to Colorado Springs and gave Jim Black one night. From there I ran to Canon City and was there from December 18 over the 23rd. There I was joined by the Aeolian Quartet, who had been touring Colorado. The quartet and this old globe-trotter left Canon City on December 24. We were now headed for Phœnix, Arizona. We spent Christmas day on the train going across Colorado and Arizona. We had one of the greatest turkey dinners we ever sat down to at the beautiful city called Las Vegas. There the train stayed long enough to give the passengers all the time they needed to eat turkey and cranberry sauce. Then we boarded the train westward bound, and about dark pulled into Albuquerque, New Mexico.

There the quartet stopped to give Brother Lee Gaines a two days' convention but I went on to Phœnix. I arrived there late in the night and was met by E. G. Roberts and wife and Brother Marvin and Sister Lillie Young. They lodged me in a good hotel and my, my, what a rest I had there for two days. The Quartet came on and joined us on Saturday and we ran over the last Sunday of December, which was the opening of the great campaign. Dr. R. T. Williams came on and joined us on Wednesday following. We ran there then over the third Sunday of January. Here we had between three and four hundred people at the altar.

When we closed there we made a run for Los Angeles. However, I stopped off two nights in Somerton where Brother E. Arthur Lewis was holding a great campaign. In his letter he tells me how many were saved each night and he said he wrote down the last night the word "Glory" after the altar service.

The last Sunday of January we opened in the First church in Los Angeles of which Dr. C. H. Babcock was pastor. Professor John E. Moore led the choir and the Aeolian Quartet sang every day. Dr. Williams and I ran over three Sundays there. We literally had hundreds of people at the altar. In these two campaigns we had 865 at the altar and we took more than one hundred people into the church out of the two conventions.

At the close of this convention I worked my way up the coast, stopping at a dozen towns for one or two days at a place. I gave Brother John B. Creighton a ten days' meeting at Selah, Washington, a few miles from Yakima. Also Brother Hepburn in Yakima two days at the close of our regular meetings. From there I made a run to Billings, Montana, and was there with Brother Kring and Brother Bennett, our District Superintendent, two days and nights.

From there I ran to Casper, Wyoming. I gave Brother Dunn three days, Friday, Saturday and Sunday, which, if my memory serves me correctly, we closed on the second Sunday of May. We ran all day on Sunday. I preached five times; Sunday school at nine, to the church at eleven, to the church at 2:30 and the young people at six and the church again at 7:30. That day we had nineteen saved and sanctified. I left there with Brother Dunn and his wife and their delegate to the District Assembly in Colorado Springs which was to meet after the second Sunday. We pulled out of Casper a little after midnight for Denver. At four o'clock Monday evening we were pulling into Denver and got supper. Brother and Sister Dunn and their delegate ran out to his brother's but I left that night on a through train for St. Louis, headed for Indianapolis.

There I joined Brother and Sister Lillenas and we had a week's convention. Brother Kenneth Wells led the singing. Brother Short was boss and general manager. At the close of this convention we put in the last week of May touring the state of Indiana, one night at a place. By June 1 I reached Cincinnati for the great campmeeting. Here were such preachers as Joseph Smith, C. W. Ruth, John and Bona Fleming, George Culp, John Knapp, M. G. Standley, Lew Standley and Brother Charles Slater. I suppose we had three hundred preachers on the ground and people saved day and night for ten days. The Cincinnati Camp is one of the greatest places in the world, to my mind.

At the close of the camp I ran down into Indiana and gave Brother Short's district one more full week. We made one town each night in the week and three towns on Sunday morning, afternoon and night. I ran back to Cincinnati. There I got a through train on Monday after the third Sunday of June and made a run from Cincinnati for Fort Lauderdale, Florida.

I preached one week in the First Church of the Nazarene. I gave two days and nights in Princeton and gave Brother Roby a week at Miami, but the weather was so warm down there that I almost lost my voice and couldn't do much. I made a run from Miami, Florida, to Lake Charles, Louisiana. There I joined our good pastor, Dr. McGraw. We had a great convention. From there I ran to Houston and gave one night in the Raymond Richie tabernacle. There were people by the multiplied hundreds. From there I joined Brother Fisher in Waco, Texas, with a great convention. Brother and Sister P. H. Lunn came down from Kansas City and Professor London was there. This was a very remarkable time.

I ran into Dallas for a night and went out and

preached at Cedar Hill. From there I made a run to Columbus, Ohio, then to Eaton Rapids, to Romeo, and from there to Gaines, then to Grand Rapids and took in the District Assembly. From Grand Rapids to Clarkesburg, Ontario, Canada. There I was joined by Professor Kenneth Wells. We held a big campmeeting there in September for good Brother Goff, who was the founder of a holiness church in that part of Canada. We had a beautiful meeting, and went from there back to Detroit and went out to the lake with the Vallayde brothers on a two days' fishing trip. This was the best time of my life. There is no finer band of brothers to go out with than the Vallayde brothers. On the trip I preached one night at Kingsville, Ontario, Canada, in the Canadian Methodist Episcopal church, which is the church home of Jack Miner, a man of nation-wide fame for what he has done with birds.

When my visit was over I made a run to Rochester, Michigan. There I went out to see the silver fox farm, where they had over seven hundred in one great farm. Ran from there to Pontiac for a couple of nights. From there I made a trip through Ohio, giving three or four short conventions, giving one week in Uhrichsville. Here we had a great campaign. From there I ran to Long island, to the New Rockaway church where Brother Paul Hill was pastor. There I joined Professor L. C. Messer and wife and we had a wonderful convention, running over two Sundays. Then we went to our school at Wollaston, Massachusetts, stopping one night in New Haven, Connecticut, and had a service with Brother L. B. Byron, one of the fine young men of the

Nazarene movement. The next day we drove in to the
Nazarene College. We gave the school the 28th, 29th
and 30th of October and had a beautiful convention.

Then I made a run back to Brooklyn and joined
Brother Morrison, Brother Zahniser, Brother Yates
and Brother Hogue. Brother and Sister Cook presided
over the Holiness Association convention. At the close
of this convention I went over and held a convention
for Brother Brown, in the old Utica Avenue church.
Brother Frank Smith of Portland, Maine, led the singing. From Brooklyn I ran down to Pittsburgh and had
two nights with Brother Brown. I ran back up the
river to a little town and joined Brother Strickland for
one night. This was a beautiful service. He put me on
the interurban at eleven o'clock and just before midnight we pulled into the union station at Pittsburgh and
on Thanksgiving morning I pulled into Chicago and
was met by Brother Chalfant and Brother Will Mc-
Pherson and another fine old Nazarene boy. We had
ten days on the north side in the Church of the Nazarene. The Lord gave us a wonderful convention. Our
Thanksgiving day and dinner were something never to
be forgotten.

Leaving Chicago for Kansas City I stopped off for
a night in First church; running through and giving a
day and night in Emporia, Kansas. From there I made
a run to Amarillo, Texas. I had a week's convention
there with Brother Dunn for whom I had held the convention in May in Casper, Wyoming. We had a great
convention in Amarillo. Leaving there I made a run
for home and stayed at home until after Christmas.

Then about the last of December I started south, reaching San Antonio and gave Brother Sharpe the last two days of December and the first few days of January, 1925. I ran from there down to Houston and joined Brother and Sister Sutton and we had a great convention for J. E. Moore, running over three Sundays. At the close of this convention I ran down to Port Arthur, and gave our good pastor, Brother Hampton, a two days' convention. Ran across from there to Lufkin, Texas, for two days with Brother Harmon; then ran over to Nacogdoches and gave Brother Smith one day. From there on up to Dallas and joined Brother Pierce, closing with him on the first day of February.

From Dallas I turned south and made a run to Gulfport, Mississippi. Stopped off with an old friend for three days and preached a half dozen times. My next stop was in Fort Lauderdale, Florida. I spent the last three weeks of February in the home of Brother and Sister Frank Davis in Fort Lauderdale. By the time I reached there I was nearly broken down. I had three weeks' rest, yet while I was there I preached twice in the First church at Lauderdale and twice down at Princeton. I gave Brother Howard Eckel in Miami one Sunday and Brother Roby on the north side one night. These three weeks spent with Brother and Sister Davis, looking at that great country, eating oranges and grapefruit, were three weeks that I will never forget in my life.

Leaving there on March 2, my next stop was Little Rock, Arkansas. There I joined Rev. John Oliver, C.

C. Rinebarger and good Sister Oliver. We worked Arkansas as it had never been worked before. We opened on March 4 and closed April 7. We made thirty towns in Arkansas and put the Herald of Holiness in three hundred and eighty homes. This was one of the greatest boosts that Arkansas had ever had. I wrote nine letters on Arkansas as the wonder state and not one unkind word or ugly criticism did I give Arkansas. One of the leading men in the state a year later said publicly that Arkansas ought to put me on a pension, for the Herald of Holiness is read around the world.

After making these thirty towns and putting Arkansas on the map for God and holiness as it had not been before I made a run to Washington, D. C. There Brother Marvin Cooper was pastor, the same dear old Marvin I had worked with in Detroit, and he had called Miss Essie Morris to lead the singing in this convention. We filled the church and ran it over, which some of them said would never be done, but it was done.

From Washington I came back to Alliance, Ohio, and gave Brother Johnson a ten days' meeting and this was a beautiful convention. From Alliance I ran across to Detroit, Michigan, again and joined Brother Willingham and had a three days' convention in First church, of which Dr. Howard Jerrett is now pastor.

On the first Sunday of May we ran over into Canada and had one great service in our church in the little city of Windsor, Ontario, Canada. From there Brother Willingham and I started west. We were now on a campaign to work for Olivet College. We stopped off for two nights in Hammond, Indiana, with Brother and Sister Turner, then made a jump to the state of Iowa, opening up in Cedar Rapids. We made twenty towns in the state, and put our school before the people and they stood by us in a most beautiful way. We came back from Iowa to the Olivet Camp. This was a very great campmeeting.

From Olivet Camp I made my way across by Cincinnati and was only there one night in 1925. Leaving Cincinnati after the night service I stopped for three days with Brother Strickland in Youngstown, Ohio. From there I ran down to Akron and gave Brother H. B. Macrory a four days' convention, closing on the first Sunday of June. From there I ran down to St. Mary's, Ohio, and gave J. C. Walker an eight days' convention. This was a very great convention. We had a big tent and then we had to sort of line up the people and preach to them by the acre. He is one great old boy.

From there I started east and stopped off one night in Baltimore where I found E. Arthur Lewis in a great campaign. From Baltimore I made a jump across by New York City and ran away up to Wolcott, Vermont. There our good Brother Manchester was in charge. We had a wonderful convention there. I made a jump from there to Manchester, New Hampshire, with Brother Mann. There I was joined by L. C. Messer and wife and his sister, Eva. We had a beautiful convention. We went from there to North Reading, Massachusetts, to the great New England District Campmeeting. My yokefellow was Brother B. F. Neely, who was at one time my pastor. The singing was in charge of Brother and Sister Lowman. This was a very great campmeeting. From there I ran across to the campmeeting at Beacon, New York. This also was a great camp, run by the New York District. My yokefellow there was Brother Lewis Reed, pastor now of First church, at Long Beach, California. We had a most beautiful campmeeting. It seems a little strange that the campmeeting committee would call two men from southern California, to the state of New York for a campmeeting. Our fellowship was sweet. We had many preachers in the camp. Brother C. B. Jernigan was District Superintendent of the New York District and was a great booster in this camp. Brother Howard Miller was District Superintendent of the New England District and he also was a booster for North Reading Camp. No finer men on earth than our good District Superintendents.

Leaving New York I ran down to Washington, D. C., and gave Marvin Cooper an all-day meeting. From Washington I joined Miss Hattie Goodrich and went down the old Potomac river to one of the old forts on the Maryland side and had a two days' convention. Coming back to Washington, I made a run to Sale City, Georgia, and joined W. W. McCord; this made the fourth time I had been with him at Sale City. He was one of the most untiring workers I have ever seen. I closed there on the last Sunday of July; leaving Monday morning.

I reached Asheville, North Carolina, Tuesday at noon. There I joined E. W. Black in the Wesleyan Methodist church and gave him four days, closing on

Friday night. My home was with Brother Lidy Crooks. There are no finer boys than the Wesleyan Methodist boys. From there I made a trip on Saturday down the mountain with a good brother in an automobile to a beautiful camp known as Camp Free at Connellys Springs, North Carolina. This was organized by Rev. Jim Green, one of the finest old boys of North Carolina. This was a very great camp. Brother John Paul of Taylor University was my yokefellow but he didn't get in for a few days after the meeting started and Brother Raymond Browning did a lot of preaching. He is one of the great preachers of the Southland.

At the close of this camp I went to Hendersonville and spent three days with Raymond Browning giving the story of my life in one of the large Baptist churches and Brother Raymond put me in his big car and drove me nearly three hundred miles over the beautiful mountains of North Carolina, to a campmeeting near the Tennessee line at Fig, North Carolina. Brother Raymond stayed with me over one Sunday. Here we had a beautiful camp. I stayed in the home of a good brother named Maxwell. From Fig a good brother took me across the country to Greensboro and we had a four days' convention. Then a good brother took me to Greer, South Carolina, and I held a camp for the Southern Methodist church there. This was the greatest campmeeting I have had for years; we had over five hundred people at the altar.

Then we made a run back north and stopped at Concord and took dinner with Brother and Sister Broom and preached at two o'clock; then made a fast drive into Thomasville and preached at night in the high school auditorium to one thousand people and stayed in the home of Brother Mason. Next day we went over to High Point and preached there afternoon and night in the Pilgrim Holiness church of which Brother Ruth was pastor. Leaving there at midnight over the north bound Southern train I pulled into Washington, D. C., the next day for breakfast and Marvin Cooper and the boys met me at the depot and we had a few hours together. My next stop was at Cambridge, Maryland. Here Brother Bean is pastor of the Pilgrim Holiness church. This was a most wonderful convention.

I made a run now from Cambridge, Maryland, to Pasadena, California, reaching home on the 26th of September. Brother Charles Slater and I had a big day in the First Church of the Nazarene. Brother Slater raised a thousand dollars for missions. Monday the 28th, Rev. Charles Slater, Brother Clark Frazier, George C. Wise and this old soldier made a run up over the mountains into the great San Jacinto valley and spent the night with Brother Frank Cooper on his great ranch. Tuesday the 29th, he put us in his big car and drove us to the giant forest. My, this was a trip. The largest known tree in the world is in this forest, the General Sherman. This tree is 36 feet and 6 inches through, 280 feet high and supposed to be not less than five thousand years old. This was one great day among those great trees. There is one rock that stands up over three thousand feet high. We made our way back into the valley that night and spent the night again with Brother Cooper and next evening drove home.

On the first Sunday of October, Dr. C. E. Hardy of Nashville, Tennessee, and I opened a convention at First Church of the Nazarene, Los Angeles, where Brother John Little was pastor. We had a great convention. At the close of this convention I made a jump to Spokane, Washington, and joined Kenneth Wells and wife and had a convention with Brother Henry Wallin in First church. There were such crowds that had to be turned away that Brother Wallin and the board planned to enlarge the church. They went to work and within six months they had a church that would seat 600 people. He is a miracle worker.

Running from Spokane to Portland, Oregon, there we joined Brother O. B. Ong and Ong and Robinson and the Wells had a two weeks' meeting with First Church of the Nazarene of which Rev. Donnell J. Smith is pastor. This was a very remarkable meeting in every way. In this campaign they also made plans to build a large, new church and already the first installment of it has been dedicated.

From there we ran up to Centralia, Washington, and joined Brother Ralph Gray. We had a great week with Brother Gray. From Centralia we came back to southern California, Robinson and the Wells holding conventions in Anaheim, Long Beach, two in Los Angeles, one or two down in the valley, one full day in First church in Pasadena, one great day with Paul Goodwin in Lamanda Park, and then stopped for Christmas. This takes us up to Christmas, 1925.

December 28 I left home for the greatest trip I

have ever made in my life. I stopped for ten days in McAllen, Texas, with Brother Clyde T. Dilley, preaching in the Southern Methodist church. Their good pastor was a brother beloved of the Lord. Leaving there Monday morning I had a run along the coast from McAllen through the beautiful orchards and gardens until we struck the beach. Then we had a full day right along the shores of the Gulf of Mexico. This was a delightful trip. I pulled into Houston at seven o'clock and was met by J. E. Moore who ran me across to the Nazarene church and had a wonderful service, then he ran me back to the depot.

At nine o'clock I got my sleeper and next morning I ate my breakfast in New Orleans. At twelve o'clock, January 12, I pulled into McComb, Mississippi, and was joined by R. H. M. Watson, our good District Superintendent. We had a beautiful convention in McComb, and from January 12 to 31 we made fifteen towns in Mississippi, many of the most beautiful towns of the state. We had two days in Jackson, two days in Hattiesburg and two days in Meridian, and we gave the other towns from one to three days. We were in Columbus three days, preaching on Sunday morning, January 31, then made a run after dinner to Tupelo and preached in the theatre in the afternoon and preached in the evening in the First Methodist, South, church where Dr. Lewis was pastor. This finished up our conventions.

Then to Georgia for February. Rev. A. B. Anderson, District Superintendent, and I toured the state. We made twenty-six towns in the month of February, preaching in ten of the largest Methodist churches in the state.

From there I made a run to Alabama. There I joined Brother H. H. Hooker, District Superintendent, and wife, Miss Essie Morris, song leader, and Miss Linis Jackson, pianist. We made twenty-seven towns in Alabama. This was a great campaign. We preached to people by the thousands. In Georgia and Alabama we put the Herald of Holiness in 600 homes.

Then I made a run to Kentucky. There I joined Brother J. W. Montgomery, District Superintendent of the Kentucky District. We made altogether twenty-seven churches in a month, preached to people by the thousands, raised three thousand dollars for home missionaries to buy tents with. This was a great campaign.

From there I made a jump to Arkansas again, opening at Batesville the first day of May. There I joined Brother Oliver, Brother Rinebarger, Sister Oliver and daughter Loraine and Paul Hill and wife; two carloads of us. Brother Rinebarger led the singing, Loraine Oliver played the piano, Sister Oliver with the Woman's Missionary Society and Brother Oliver raised money and Bud Robinson did most of the preaching. During this time we made thirty-three cities. This makes the second time I have toured Arkansas. I ran from there to Olivet Camp for the last week of May and then to Cincinnati for the first week of June. I came from there to Pasadena, reaching home on June 10 and had four days in the District Assembly.

CHAPTER XVI

Professor L. C. Messer and I had planned a trip to Canada, so he left his home in Durant, Oklahoma, on Monday, June 7, in his big Willys-Knight car. He and his wife reached Pasadena the same day that I reached home. We left Pasadena on June 15 and worked our way clear north to Red Deer, Alberta, Canada. We gave one night in Rich Grove, California, one night in Lindsay, one night in Fresno, one in Stockton, two in Sacramento, one in Medford, one in Portland, Oregon, one in The Dalles, Oregon, one in Yakima, Washington, one in Walla Walla, Washington, two nights in Spokane, Washington, and left Spokane on Monday the 28th, headed now for Canada. At noon we went through King's Gate at Eastport and traveled for two hundred miles on the western slope of the Canadian Rockies. On that Rocky Mountain trip we went by Columbia lake, out of which the great Columbia river flows that makes a big curve and crosses the line into the United States and makes the dividing line between Washington and Oregon and out into the ocean. We went through the Canadian National Park and saw the great moose, the deer and the Rocky Mountain goats.

We gave three days in Calgary, Alberta, for Roy Smee in the First Church of the Nazarene and July 2 we drove into Red Deer. Brother O. B. Ong was my yokefellow here. In ten days we had five hundred

people at the altar. This is one of the greatest camps
that I have been in for a number of years. At the close
of the camp Brother and Sister Messer ran back to
Calgary, and I ran over to Edmonton for one night.
Our trip was beautiful and we had a wonderful service.
Boarded the train at midnight and was back for breakfast next morning in Calgary. Edmonton is the capital
of Alberta and a most beautiful city but my recollection
is that Calgary is larger and more beautiful.

Here we turned east and made a thousand-mile
run. We stopped and preached one night in Morse,
one night in Medicine Hat, one night in Moose Jaw and
went on to Regina, the capital of Saskatchewan. Our
yokefellows here were Brother Jones and Brother Metcalf. No finer boys living. Brother Metcalf was edu-
cated in Pasadena College and Brother Jones in Bethany-Peniel College of Oklahoma. When we closed in
Regina we went through the greatest wheat fields I
have seen in my life. We saw wheat that made eighty
bushels per acre; as far as your eyes could see it was
wheat fields.

We drove out through southern Canada and crossed
the line between Canada and Montana to Miles City
and spent the night. They claim that Miles City is the
largest horse market in the known world. Next night
we drove to Billings, Montana, and preached in the
First Church of the Nazarene and had a most beautiful
service. Our good pastor had just arrived a week before from the Washington-Philadelphia District but
was getting a fine start. Next morning we were up

early and made a run for Yellowstone National Park.

We drove in at noon and drove all through the park by the next afternoon. We did not stay long at each place. Drove out at the west gate and drove that night to Idaho Falls, eating supper and going to bed at midnight. Next night we drove into Boise. There we joined Brother Sanner, Dr. Morrison, Brother and Sister Aycock and a host of other fine workers. There were nearly four hundred at the altar during this meeting. Closing on August 8 and leaving August 9, we preached on Monday night at Pocatello, Idaho, Tuesday night at Salt Lake City, Wednesday night at Grand Junction, Colorado, Thursday in Canon City, Colorado, Friday night in Dalhart, Texas, Saturday night we reached the campmeeting at Dodsonville, Texas. Here Brother and Sister Ellis were in charge. When I got there my old friend of twenty-five years, A. D. Buck, was in charge. We ran for ten days and we had hundreds of people from at least three hundred miles distant, from Texas and New Mexico. This camp was one of glory and power, although we were well-nigh rained out at times, but God was on the scene.

At the close at Dodsonville we turned the nose of our great car east and stopped one night in Joplin, Missouri, one night in Iberia, Missouri, and one night in St. Louis.

Our next stop was at Columbus, Indiana. My yokefellow was Rev. H. N. Dickerson and Professor Messer in charge of the music. This was a beautiful camp. At the close of this camp we decided to take a

few days' rest, but as we had to go east we drove out
through eastern Indiana and to Toledo, Ohio, left our
big car to have some work done and ran into Detroit
for one night, then to Pontiac, Michigan, and had a
week's rest. We gave them one Sunday in the Nazarene
church.

From Pontiac we ran back into Toledo, got our car
and drove on east, spending that night in Cleveland.
Driving the next night into Rochester, New York,
where we had a two days' convention, then into Syracuse for a two days' convention, then to Brooktondale
for a day and night and joined H. V. Miller, District
Superintendent of the New England District, and made
a run to Springfield, Massachusetts, where we had one
beautiful night. From there we ran to Keene, New
Hampshire; from Keene, we crossed to Leicester, Vermont; from there to Waterville, Vermont; from there
to Hill West; from there to Johnston, Vermont; from
there to Wolcott, Vermont; from there we made a run
to Jackman, Maine; from there to Auburn, Maine;
then to Bath, Maine; from there we went to Portland,
Maine; giving one night to South Portland and one
morning and afternoon to First church in Portland and
back to South Portland at night.

Our next stop was Livermore Falls, Maine, and our
next stop was Haverhill, Mass. Here we have a great
church with a great pastor. Then we made another
trip into New Hampshire stopping in Derry for one
night, where we have a beautiful new church and had a
good time. Next in Fitchburg, Massachusetts. Here

Brother Arthur Ingler was in charge. Our next stop was in Worcester, Massachusetts. Here we have a beautiful work, a new church organized in the summer. From there we ran down to South Manchester, Connecticut. There we had a great time and went from there to Danielson, Connecticut. We had a great service there and God was on hand to bless. Our next stop was in New Bedford, Massachusetts, with Jimmie Kirkland. This was a wonderful service. From there we ran to Cambridge and had one night with G. E. Waddle, one of the most beautiful men in the world. Next night we were in Everett, Massachusetts. This was a most beautiful service. From there we ran over to the college at Wollaston and had a five days' convention. It was a great convention.

At the close of this we turned the nose of our great car southward and in one day we passed through Massachusetts, Connecticut, Rhode Island, New Jersey, New York and a good portion of Pennsylvania. We camped that night twenty-five miles below Philadelphia and drove up to Washington next morning in time for breakfast. At Washington's old home we had the pleasure of seeing Queen Marie of Rumania, also her son and daughter. We took supper that night in Richmond, Virginia, drove on twenty-five or thirty miles down the highway and put up for the night. Drove into Greensboro, North Carolina, the next night and preached. The next day we drove into Charlotte, North Carolina, and preached at night. Next night we drove into Atlanta, Georgia. Here we took in the District

Assembly and stayed a week longer and had a most beautiful convention.

At the close of our beautiful convention in Atlanta with Brother Anderson and Brother Simmons, we made a run northwest; spending one night in the northeast corner of Mississippi with Brother Messer's aunt; spending the next night in Little Rock, Arkansas, with Lee Gaines, the pastor; we spent the next night in Antlers, Oklahoma, in the home of the Isbell family, the mother of Sister Messer.

Leaving Sister Messer there with her mother, Professor Messer and I drove on to Dallas, Texas, and joined our pastor, Brother Parks, on November 5, running over the 14th. This was a most beautiful convention. All of the afternoon and night services were held in the Haskell Avenue Methodist church of which Rev. Robert Thompson, a beautiful Scotch brother, was pastor.

Leaving there on Sunday night, the 14th, we drove through to Durant by 5:30 the next morning, getting three hours' sleep and driving to Henryetta for the night. Rev. Allie Irick was opening a great campaign. I preached one night, November 15, and Tuesday I left Brother Irick and Brother Messer in the thick of the fight and made a run to Kansas City and stopped over two nights with the boys at the Publishing House.

Then I made a jump to Charleston, West Virginia, held a ten days' meeting in the great Union Mission of which Brother Pat P. Withrow is superintendent. This is one of the greatest and most beautiful missions I have ever worked in. Their buildings are probably worth a half million dollars. My stay with Brother Withrow could not have been more pleasant. I preached twice while there in the great Central Methodist church; went up the river one day and preached one afternoon in a beautiful Baptist church for Dr. Smith, but was back at the mission in time for the night service.

From there I made a jump into southeast Oklahoma and joined Brother S. H. Owens, the District Superintendent, Professor L. C. Messer and his father and we opened a tour for the district in Poteau. We began December 1 in Poteau and closed December 19 in Durant. We made seventeen towns in these nineteen days. This was an unusually interesting trip. We were in such cities as Poteau, Muskogee, Tulsa, Sapulpa, Collinsville, Bartlesville, Hominy, Shawnee, Henryetta, Holdenville, Atwood, Ada, Tishomingo, Madill, Hugo, Antlers, and finished up in Durant.

This brought us to December 19. In 1926 I worked in forty-two states, three provinces of Canada, preached nearly five hundred times and put the Herald of Holiness in 2800 homes. I wrote the "Good Samaritan Chats" every week and the closing of my year's work of 1926 completes forty-seven years of religious work. During this time I have traveled just about one million miles, have preached 18,000 times. I have prayed with more than 80,000 people at the mourner's bench and have traveled and worked the United States like it was a field, and have worked four provinces of

Canada. Up to the present I have written thirteen books. They have sold by the tens of thousands and the end is not yet. This date finds this old preacher blood-red, sky-blue, snow-white, straight as a gun stick and red-hot. May the blessings of heaven rest upon every man, woman and child that may read this book. I send it forth loaded to the water line with the activities of forty-seven years of labor in the kingdom of the Lord Jesus Christ.

Faithfully yours,

Bud Robinson.

Recd 1932.

CPSIA information can be obtained
at www.ICGtesting.com
Printed in the USA
LVHW110219010719
622830LV00001B/5/P